A BEGINNER'S GUIDE TO CHRISTIAN MEDITATION

JOURNEYING INTO THE HEART OF THE DIVINE

A BEGINNER'S GUIDE TO CHRISTIAN MEDITATION
Journeying into the heart of the Divine

Taylor Remington

A BEGINNER'S GUIDE TO CHRISTIAN MEDITATION - Journeying into the heart of the Divine
Copyright © 2020 Rooakh

www.rooakh.com

Published by Seraph Creative
First Edition
ISBN 978-0-6486986-1-6

Christian Meditation, Christian spirituality, mysticism, transformation, contemplation, personal growth, prayer.

Scripture quotations from the New American Standard Bible, unless otherwise stated.

Cover art by Taylor Remington

Typesetting & Layout by Feline

www.felinegraphics.com

TABLE OF CONTENTS

*Dedicated to my amazing wife
and best friend, Megan.*

Many more journeys await us.

FOREWORD

Of all the students that began with me a few years after I arrived in Venice California, Taylor and his now wife Megan have been among the most persistent and studious practitioners. Taylor, the author of this book, is an authentic practitioner and student of the mysteries. This book serves as an introduction to meditation from a Christian perspective, and yet is useful for anyone from any background who is interested in mind, body, and soul development. The work establishes and lays out structures and processes of mediation that are easy to follow, yet profoundly spiritual. It is not easy to write a book that is both scholastically thorough and spiritually personable on any given day. Taylor has managed to do so in the following chapters, which are indeed well-researched and well-presented. From the beginning to the end, it describes for the beginner basic historic and theoretical ideas informing mediation interspersed with authentic spiritual experiences coming from the author's own inner well. Taylor has not only studied spirituality, he experiments and experiences. This work, as a result, is an integration of various practices.

How can we catch the speedy wind of the movements of the faster light flashes of the realm of the spirit? Or rather how do we make ourselves available for its waves to sweep us into its ethereal currents? Those flashy currents that dance past the peripheral of our oh-so-busy minds...how do we steady them and use them as a door into the inner landscape of the spirit? The answer is through meditation. Very few of us are gifted with the native capacity to hold the attention in that realm. Even those who have that gift, natively, must learn how to hold those experiences steady, drawing from their beauty and sometimes terror in such a way that they come out the other side and those experiences become a kaleidoscope of wonderful spectrums of divine light. Everyone must learn, and the best way to learn is through the practice of meditation. Most beginners and even veterans often wonder at the fauna of consciousness and other realms without taking hold of self-transformation. Sometimes all that is needed is guidance in order to enter and sustain the seeker through practices until one can find the way to their own garden. This book on meditation, I believe, will do that. Taylor has produced a work that I believe can help both the novice and the veteran in their journey. This is a needed book, and thank God it is also very well-written and articulated. I recommend this book with gratitude to God. It will be a blessing to anyone who takes it up and pays attention.

Adonijah O. Ogbonnaya, Ph.D
Venice, California 2020

"The Ecology of Heaven is like a grain of mustard seed, which a human took and sowed in his field, which indeed is the least of all seeds: but when it is grown, it is the greatest among herbs and becomes a tree, so that the birds of the air come and lodge in the branches thereof."

Matthew 13:31-32

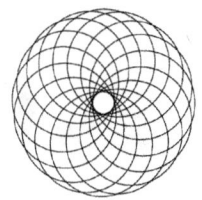

INTRODUCTION

My journey in meditational processes began about eight years ago, and it is from the experiences and learning during this time that this book has emerged. It has been formed from my desire to see individuals and communities in Christianity explore and practice meditational activities in order to awaken to deeper realities of our Spiritual union with Christ. Almost a decade ago, I started to explore my Jewish roots and began to experiment with various Jewish techniques as prescribed and taught by my teacher and mentor Adonijah Ogbonnaya PhD., a Nigerian Jewish-Christian theologian and mystic.[i] By implementing and practicing such processes, I began to notice the subtleties of the mind-body connection, which play a large role in the way we can access certain Spiritual worlds in transpersonal states of consciousness.

As time went on and my practice deepened, I sought out Christian techniques that I could use and integrate from different eras in the last two millennia. During this search, I found helpful stories and examples of methods but there were few resources on "how-to's" of proper engagement for non-monastics. With the help of the Spirit, I was able to experiment with and refine techniques and methodologies, and discovered through trial and error that they had an intensifying effect on my spiritual engagements. This book is filled with the foundational tools that I used and still continue to use in order to engage the Holy Spirit, to awaken the reality of my union with Christ, and to move into meta-worlds and systems with the intention of "bringing heaven to earth." These techniques have led and continue to lead me to experience various trans-somatic states,[ii] ecstatic states of union, words of knowledge, prophetic insights, heart transformations, emotional and somatic balancing, relational restoration and much more.

One of the keys to this type of spiritual work that I have learned is to keep one's heart and mind focused on the presence of the Holy Spirit that springs forth within like a fountain. Here within, we find the gateway to the living water that sustains and gives life to the Soul. I experienced this gateway some time ago in the middle of the night, when I woke up and felt an energetic presence in the room. I laid in bed and began my practice of bringing attention to my breath and engaged focus with the presence I felt around me. After a short time, I heard a voice say, "Get up and walk." At that moment, I experienced something like in the movie Doctor Strange when Stephen Strange is pushed out of his body by his teacher and I found myself floating and completely outside myself. This was not in my imagination or in my mind in any capacity — I was outside myself completely and 100% awake, conscious, lucid, and aware. It was not a dream-state or lucid dream but an out-of-body experience. Now, I must note that when this happened I was visiting a location I had never been to before and arrived late at night so I had not seen what was outside or around the area. When I looked up, I saw Jesus standing and glowing in a pure radiant light and he said, "Follow me. I have something to show you." As he walked through the wall to the outside, I followed him through the wall where I saw the "outside" garden. The various plants I was viewing as I was floating around in the garden area were not only colorfully vibrant under the moonlit ambience but the outside of the leaves were filled with pulsating other-worldly golden light. As we floated down, he led me to a fountain in the middle of the garden and said to me, "Drink." I floated down, got down on my knees, and took my spiritual hands, cupped the water and took a drink; at the moment of my sip I instantaneously zapped back into my body. The next morning, I got up and the outside world I had never seen before was nearly identical to what I had seen outside myself — except for the glowing golden leaves. The only major difference was that the fountain was not there physically, but was a spiritual component overlaid upon the world I was in.

Through that experience, I learned that the continual drinking of the presence leads one to experience a deeper communion with Christ that not only brings about the transformative nature of Christ within, but also leads to various states of consciousness that allow one to access dimensional worlds of Divine presence. However, I quickly learned that drinking of the presence wasn't always easy because my mind was easily distracted. The key to all of this comes down to one's focus or gaze. Thus, the techniques in this book are to help you fine-tune your mind in order to enhance and sensitize your gaze upon the indwelling presence of Christ.

Do not be discouraged if nothing happens right away. I have gone through long seasons where it was very difficult for me to focus, or I just wasn't having anything profound happening. But when things started to open up again spiritually, I was able to see how the processes I was continuing to practice in the dry seasons were carrying me along and preparing me for what I was about to awaken to next. So, take heart — know that this is a journey, a process into the heart of the Divine. Like Abraham, we are nomads.Our home lies in the reality of becoming, growing, and following the life and movement of the Spirit. And these processes are part of that journey that bring us ever closer to a continual awakening of the Divine presence within.

As we move forward on our journeys, we now find that a new world is upon us as we move forward into a new era of Christian Spiritual practice and its emerging participation with the Divine Spirit. This book aims to lay the ground work for some practices that will lead to greater communion with the Spirit, but, before delving into such methods of meditation, spiritual practices, and the imagination, I must note a few key terminological adjustments used throughout this work.

Firstly, I refer to God in its unified collective character as "the Divine" in the pages ahead. Its etymology leans toward that which is characteristically manifested of the highest ideals of Spirit. The activity or energy of the Divine I call "Spirit." It conveys the movement and life of the Trinity that interpenetrates the whole of creation and its inter-relationality that draws all activity into flowing moments of loving unification and restoration.[iii] I try to avoid using the name "God" not because I do not believe in the word but rather because "God," in our traditional understanding of that word, references only one aspect of the Divine. Depending on how one approaches its etymology, it may be related to the "good" or "to pour," as in pour a libation towards. Intentional, creative purposes highlight other names, and therefore have the potential to broaden our experience by broadening our vocabulary when referencing "God."

Secondly, I have chosen to use the term "Ecology of the Spirit" in lieu of the traditional translation "Kingdom of God." I am by no means against using the word "kingdom" or even "Kingdom of God," however, my sense is that there is a more meaning-full term for us today that I believe reflects the depth of meaning that Jesus expressed in the Gospels. In order to understand the reasoning behind this word substitution, we must first examine the term "ecology." The Greek word or prefix *eco* means "house or environment," which implies a familial connection between members of a shared environ. Next, the suffix *logia* means "study of, x" and it is worth noting that logia is related to the Greek word Logos, meaning "Word." This does not mean that we should bring to mind the written Bible but rather the context in which the Gospel of John calls Jesus the Logos; this refers to that which gives structures and form to all life. It is the mind or consciousness of the Spirit made manifest in order to produce difference and multiplicity, allowing for distinctions to be made, thus "All things came into being through Him, and apart from Him nothing came into being that has come into being." Simply put, whenever you see the word "ecology" in this book, it refers to the environmental, creative, and loving process of the Word-Logos.

This ecological terminology brings our symbolic sensemaking[iv] back to its relational vision of its naming. Through such shifts, we are brought back into a familial image that reconfigures our attention to the Cosmos and our redeemed role with all Nature as co-participators, that is, of be-ing benefactors and caretakers of this Creation. Such an ecology that Jesus, or in Hebrew Yeshua, calls us to seek, then, is not an abstract or distant image of "ruling" but rather highlights our incredible role in the process of sustaining, producing and restoring all forms of life.

Furthermore, and purposefully so, the environmental imagery of this term enhances the statement of Yeshua in John 3 that the Spirit is like the wind, breath, and air that moves, shapes, creates, and fills the entire world. For just as the air we breathe gives our body life, the Ecology of the Spirit is the life of our entire Be-ing. And just as the breath or wind is invisible yet its impact and actions are seen through the visible creation, the Ecology of the Spirit manifests and makes known the action of Spirit within the world, through our actions and the all-encompassing aspects of the Good, True, Beautiful, and Love. This is how the Ecology of the Spirit is made known.

The word "environment," I am aware, is provocatively earth-centric. It is intentionally symbolically rooted in our relationship to creation and all of its processes in which the Heaven(s) play their part. I am certainly not saying that we should ignore the Heaven(s) or neglect the pursuit of exploration of those arenas in our spiritual practices — may it never be! By all means, let us ascend or (in)scend into realms wherein the Spirit's immanence of presence is intensified. But remember: our experiences should translate into ways that steward life for all people and all creation. Indeed, the heavens and the Earth are entangled in the Ecology of the Spirit and are not wholly separate realties, but rather immanent to yet distinct manifestations from the creativity of the Spirit (Gen. 1:1).

Each of the following chapters in this guidebook are accompanied by a short exercise or activation, to which I encourage you to return often and integrate into your own practices. I recommend digesting the reading slowly and taking time for each exercise and activation, allowing them to sink into your mind and body. This book is not meant to be read in an hour, but over time and with practical application. In terms of content, chapter one examines why meditational practices are centrally important for Christian practice moving forward. Chapter two considers the quality of be-ing that emerges through meditational practice, while chapter three provides a brief overview of what meditation entails and unpacks some of the physiological benefits for its uses. Next, chapter four explores the ways in which the ancient Israelites practiced meditation, while chapter five briefly overviews the historical processes of early Christian meditational practices. Chapter six discusses the ways in which our bodies become spiritual antennas in meditation. Chapter seven provides an introduction into mind(full) practice and centering prayer, and chapter eight elucidates how the image sensorium—the place where the mind "sees"—operates. Chapters nine and ten delve into the apophatic process of mystical ascent and the ways in which we can center our gaze on the Presence, respectively, and chapter eleven presents a brief overview of the breath and its role in our meditational practice. Lastly, chapter twelve includes my closing thoughts and parting encouragements.

So friends, let us be transformed by our mystical pursuits in Christ and its ever-increasing joy, but let us not forget that Christ has called us to seek the Ecology of the Spirit. This is not for the mere enjoyment of heavenly experiences but to transform the world into its own version or creative vision that hearkens to the environs of the Heaven(s). As we engage the world of Christian meditation and the aspects of spiritual technologies in the chapters ahead, let us not forget that our union with Christ that emerges through our practices will inevitably lead to the transformations of our lives, both local and cosmic.

"And the Divine said to the soul:
I desired you before the world began.
I desire you now
As you desire me.
And where the desires of the two come together
There love is perfected."

- Mechthild of Magdeburg

1

LOOKING AHEAD

Many in the church are asking, "Why are so many young people (or people in general) leaving the church? When/how will they return? How do we engage those who are opting out?" Part of the problem for the church today is that most humans under the age of thirty five, and many others of all age groups, are no longer blindly accepting life-restricting ideas on the collective subconscious level. As the human is being transformed by the Spirit from glory to glory, old wineskin types of theologies^v and entertainment based systems are not embedding well into the emerging human psyche and as a result, the majority of institutions or churches that uphold these ideas are no longer seeing attendees return. So then, what *are* these new minds interested in? Among many things, they are interested in inclusive spiritualities, ideas that develop compassion for the environment, and practices that enable personal experiences of the immanent Spirit.

The old fear tactics that would have kept many in church pews are losing grip as more people now have access to the historical roots of these doctrines and can research for themselves. If fear won't work anymore, then what will? Perhaps we should consider a mystical revolution that is rooted in compassion, love, inclusivity, and *participatory dimensions of practice,* which is the summative heart of the work you hold in your hands. We cannot merely stand in front of the church for hours on end and endlessly teach. We must engage in both communal *and* individually stewarded participation so we may enter into the palpable experience of the Ecology of the Spirit. From this place we can then begin to invite others into the participatory reality of being a Christ-ian, that is, of flowing and participating in the Divine flow of one-ness.

Ideas of the previous wineskins that are founded on static and non-participatory values have enabled shallow renderings of the message and life of Jesus and produced entertainment-based church spectacles, which will inevitably break down. Instead of being entertained by those with the microphone, we are making the move to partake of the spiritual reality and its unfolding in each of our lives. This shift will, among many other things, re-introduce to seeking Christians different types of meditational and contemplative practices as well a refining of the practicing and workings of the gifts of the Spirit. On one level, this deeper participation in the gifts of the Spirit allows us to become acquainted with transpersonal and visional activities of the mind. This will inevitably lead to questions, seeking, and knocking. Sounds like the process Jesus repeatedly describes! It wont always be pretty, as few processes ever are, but there is something rapidly emerging within us that is pushing us beyond our comfortable boundaries and conventions. I invite you to be willing to innovate, be open to change, and to accept mystery as we approach a new epoch in participatory and experiential modalities together.

In sum, this small book was written to aid you in your journey into the participatory dimension of Christian meditation and spiritual practice. I hope that it helps to guide you in practice and perhaps give understanding to a few of the many questions that arise as one begins to have mystical experiences. At the same time, I also hope that it creates more questions in the process that answers are discovered. This brief introduction is not intended to be an overview of Christian mysticism or Christian mystical theology by any means, but rather as a guidebook to assist you in situating yourself in relation to the foundations of Christian meditation. By not focusing on supplicative or desire-based prayer as the primary means of meditation, we can make space for and begin the practice of various techniques that allow oneself to flow in union with Christ within. As a blessing, may you be evermore transformed in the love of the Divine for the purpose of continually re-imagining the human and its relation to all in Christ.

"And be not conformed to this world: but be transformed by the renewing of your mind, that you may prove what is that good, and pleasing and harmonious, will of the Spirit."

Romans 12:2

2

NEW INTER-REALITIES

The natural body, according to traditions of some mystical Jewish communities, unfolds from at least forty components or nodes of spatial folding, which form a twelve or sixteen-dimensional projection that reveals the physical world in our three- dimensional space.[vi] One can think of them as forty points of light that refract in order to produce a holographic yet very real world. From this embodied experience, one's mind shapes and is shaped by the garment of reality as experienced within one's space time world. Each plane or world is incredibly thin. However, the mind as infinite space allows the construction of any given plane to unfold within its certain patterns of construction, and within that world the physicality is real. It is felt, seen, heard and fundamentally experienced, like even in a dream, but still a part of the mind.

The mind is fundamentally attracted to and behaves under certain laws and conditions in order to "stay" within this planeral space sphere. Through meditation, sleeping, and altered states in general, however, those laws may bend or break, which allows one to experience alternative realities or worlds or conditions of be-ing. That is not to say that one should ignore this world or seek its escape in order to leave all creatures behind. Rather one should seek a harmonious re-conditioning of one's nature in order to transform, heal, and deliver insights to the creatures within their world. The book of Philippians and Hebrews state that Jesus emptied himself of His God-nature in order to take on the human—in other words, Jesus took on the conscious condition to inhabit and experience this world in its current form.[vii] And when he walked among us, He did not leave us right away, but rather introduced to us prescriptive and demonstrative behavioral actions that would transform our world. He fully embedded His mark within this world even after His resurrection. It is this very notion that we should remember when we seek and enter into mystical experiences. They are not solely for our enjoyment but for the betterment of the entire cosmos. Every insect, rock, bee, flower, plant, animal, and neighbor benefits from our transformation and awakening.

The question arises then...how does one start? Where does one begin? That answer is simple: "Seek ye first the Ecology of the Spirit and all of these things will be added unto you." Where should one seek this ecological domain? Again, the reply is simple: "The Ecology of Divine is within you." The journey is first within the sphere of the heart, as the subtitle of this work highlights. We must seek and discover what one is and to forfeit every thing that blocks the path to one's freedom in the Ecology of the Spirit. The rubric to one's discovery or prerequisites for beginning this ecological work cannot be found within a set list of doctrines or magical prayers, but rather is manifested through a quality of be-ing, which is quite simple:

> *If I speak with the tongues of humans and of angels, but do not*
> *have love, I have become a noisy gong or a clanging cymbal. If*

I have the gift of prophecy, and know all mysteries and all knowledge; and if I have all faith, so as to remove mountains, but do not have love, I am nothing. And if I give all my possessions to feed the poor, and if I surrender my body to be burned, but do not have love, it profits me nothing. (1 Corinthians 13:1-3)

But the fruit of the Spirit is love, joy, peace, patience, kindness, goodness, faithfulness, gentleness, and self-control. (Galatians 5:22)

These qualities are not to be forcibly created or projected within oneself, nor should we label those who have patterns of destructive behavior as "on the outside." Instead, one should be fundamentally patient, kind, and gentle with oneself and others on this journey. No one "gets it" right away. This is our lifetime of journeying, processing, and transforming with the Spirit. With this in mind, legalism and behavioralism can be completely dissolved in the lives of those who seek the Ecology of the Spirit. For since we are present in all, we should seek to liberate others from suffering through any sort of harmony, compassion, love, and generosity to the degree that one is able. The letter to the Galatians describes this as "bearing one another's burdens" (Gal. 6:2). This does not mean that all need to become social workers or live in a monastery, but rather we should all aim to adjust the condition of the world through the smallest of acts of love, according to the degree and gift that one is able. Over time, this practiced, transformative outlook positions the heart to seek a perpetual flow of giving, for others, serving, teaching, healing, and time-spending. There are an infinite amount of ways this explosion of selfless energy can emerge. Indeed, it can be seen in the breast-feeding of a mother, the teaching of a father, or the sharing with one's neighbor. We should be careful to not make static characterizations of what we deem as spiritual or "holy," but instead seek what is beneficial and life-giving. From that place, the activities of the Ecology of the Spirit are endless.

Lastly, not only are the *activities* endless, but so are the *personas* or the personal expressions. The diversity of potential characterizations should be sought, encouraged, and celebrated. Some individuals will be mild-mannered, while others full of energy, zeal, and excitement. There will be extroverts, introverts, and everywhere in between. All of the differentiations that we see within the world among the human population in the parameters of loving-ness and harmonious-ness are but personal refections of the possible expressions and manifestations of the Divine.

As the aspects or qualities of the soul[viii] begin to emerge through the activity of the Spirit which flows, transforms, and reconditions one's be-ing, one is brought into perpetual ec-stasis, that is, one is constantly being shifted outside of oneself. This process of novel infusion re-imagines the human potential both in an individual and collective sense. This loving foundation is essential to the practices and techniques discussed in the pages ahead.

"Abide in Me, and I AM in you. As the branch cannot bear fruit of itself unless it abides in the vine, so neither can you unless you abide in Me.

I AM the vine, you are the branches; he who abides in the I AM and Me in him, he bears much fruit, for apart from the I AM you can do nothing."

John 15:4-5

3

FOUNDATIONS OF MEDITATION

When you think about meditation, what comes to your mind first? Did you imagine a man sitting and chanting? Was your mind blank? Did you think about nuns singing and chanting hymns? Meditation is a term that covers a wide range of practices and mindsets for living. The truth is, anything that is done intentionally with focus and conscious energy is a type of meditation. Meditation is not a process of falling asleep, but rather one in which we become more awake or attuned to ourselves' Self in Christ. So, even walking, eating, breathing, stretching, working, or anything done in a spirit of care-full wakefulness and watchfulness is a type of meditation. There are some that assume the goal of meditation is to "empty" one's mind. Although there are times that one should clear their mind, one is never truly "emptying" it. It is important to note however that when the mind clearing does occur, one can fill it with the Presence. Again, the goal isn't to empty but to intentionally focus or bring one's be-ing into a place of peace. And as we will discuss throughout this book, meditation is much more nuanced and complex than the simple idea that it is all about "emptying" one's mind.

So, what is the purpose of meditation? Meditation moves one's being into a mode where one becomes sensitive to the activity of Divine presence. Although one may not be initially "sensitive" to that presence, the activity of meditation itself slowly transforms and retunes the faculties of sensing to be able to feel and sense the Divine presence. When this Divine presence is felt within one's being, one should continually focus or abide their attention upon that presence for as long as one is able to so. Within this practice of focusing one's being on the Presence one begins to enter into an abiding aspect of communion. In this alternate dimension of taking communion, the bread and the wine become the *energia* itself of the Divine presence that is becoming actualized through focused awareness. The *energia* of the Holy Spirit moves and shifts the various aspects of one's mind, heart, and subtle bodies in order to bring them into a place of harmony and wholeness.

Practically speaking, meditation has many well-documented benefits as well. Since the 1970s, a number of studies have been performed that explore the somatic and psychological impacts of various types of meditation.[ix] What has been discovered over the years is that there are a number of health benefits that are produced, stimulated, and maintained through the practice of sitting meditation. These benefits include positive impacts on blood pressure, cancer,[x] hypertension[xi] and the ease of chronic pain[xii] Furthermore, it helps strengthen the immune system to defend against colds and the flu.[xiii]

In addition to the somatic benefits there are also many positive psychological benefits which include improved concentration and attention, improved memory and intelligence, better sleep, as well as decreased anxiety, stress and depression.[xiv] All of these studies have shown that consistent meditators are happier, more content[xv] and as a result have longer and healthier lives.[xvi] What one can conclude from this research is that the journey and integration of meditation into the life of the Human across the world has only begun.[xvii] There are, of course, other cultures and regions of the world where the practice of meditation is already ingrained and integrated within the community at large and has been for centuries, if not millennia. Although for many areas of the globe like the modern, Anglo-Saxon West, various meditational practices are becoming noticed and studied anew for their health benefits, both physical and psychological. As a result, they are becoming more and more integrated into the daily lives of those seeking its transformative capacities.

As you move forward through this book, you will see various exercises at the end of each chapter. I highly recommend that you take the time to participate in each practice, as they are the life-blood of this book. Anytime you see that one of the exercises calls for sitting and relaxing, I recommend the following tips:

Find a physical place that you go back to each time you meditate in order to create a sort of sacred space in your living area. This helps to bring you back into the flow of your practice each time you sit down. Furthermore, if you are feeling stressed you know you can go back to this place at any time to bring a sense of relaxation to the soul and body, much like the "prayer closet" that Jesus describes in Matthew 6:6.

- Sit up straight if you are sitting down. It is best to use a chair that allows you to sit up straight but is still comfortable. Ideally, you want to have your feet flat on the ground as you sit in the chair. By sitting up straight you are opening electrical meridians and blood vessels in your body that help one to relax, heal, restore, and rejuvenate. If you choose to lie down, just make sure your back is straight as you lie down on your back.

- Make sure you do not cross your legs or arms. If you are cold, get comfortable, put on a sweatshirt, or place a blanket over your legs. It is important to not cross in order keep this posture of openness for your system.

- If you prefer to sit on the ground make sure your back is straight and that, again, you find yourself in a comfortable position. For beginners, I do recommend getting a pillow or cushioned rug to sit on to aid one's sitting. It will help one to not get focused on the discomfort one is feeling but will allow one to get in the flow of the practice instead.

- Again, be comfortable! If you need to move a little as you are sitting, a slight adjustment here or there, that is okay! Listen to your body.

- It is more than reasonable to throw on relaxing music in the background if that is something that helps you focus and calm yourself. It isn't necessary but if this is something that helps you calm down, go for it!

- If the exercise calls for noticing the breath or has some sort breath-work to it, I recommend breathing in through the nose and out through the mouth or nose. When you inhale, try to breathe in from the belly first and up through the chest so as to lift your entire diaphragm. In this way, you are inhaling not just from the lungs but using your entire diaphragm to breathe, which helps in energizing your organs that exist in your belly and lower diaphragm.

So far, we have seen that there are many benefits of meditation for one's body and mental health, as well as practical tips for effective meditation. In addition to these, there are of course dynamic, spiritual aspects that help to train oneself to circumvent the "ego," and release the Spirit and its work within our lives. These spiritual realities can be expressed within the following questions, which I encourage you to ponder:

Who am I?

Who is the Divine?

How might I transform my heart?

How do I become more self-less?

How do I become attuned to and in vibration with the Ecology of Heaven?

How might I get to truly know the Life of Christ within me?

What does Christ in me *feel* like?

What does it feel like to have the Spirit flow in, around, and through me?

How might I release the image of Christ in my day to day life?

Opening Exercise: 10 minutes

Sit quietly for a moment and ask yourself one of the above
questions listed or a question of your own. I recommend
beginning with the first two. Who am I? Who is the Divine?
What is my purpose in meditational practice? Observe your
answers. Be gentle and compassionate with yourself. There
are no right or wrong answers. Your answers are disclosing
the depths of your be-ing and the structures that are created
within. As you conclude, however many moments later, tell
yourself and the Holy Spirit "thank you." Return to this
exercise every few months, since this is not intended to be a
one-time exercise. This should become a ritual[xviii], discipline or
"practice," of sorts that one may implement every few months.

"...but YHVH was not in
the fire.

And after the fire came
a still, small voice
[breath]."

1 Kings 19:11-12

"Hear, O Israel! YHVH our Elohim,
YHVH is one!

You shall love YHVH your Elohim with
all your heart and with all your soul
and with all your might."

Deuteronomy 6:4-5

4

HEBREW LANGUAGE AND BIBLICAL CONTEXT FOR MEDITATION

Before considering the linguistic and biblical bases for meditation, we must note that most biblical ideas of spiritual practice fall under the heading of "prayer.» These can be expressed in many ways, such as those calling upon the Divine Names throughout the Psalter or one putting their head between their knees in order to induce a certain state as Elijah at Carmel (1 Kings 18:42). Because of our religious ideals and the way were taught or trained within our Christian practices, many of us were never shown the various spiritual dimensions or practices that were a part of the ancient Israelite (and later Jewish) tradition from which Christianity sprung. Remember, Jesus and his earliest followers were Jewish and remained so. By bringing our attention to the languages of the Bible — both Hebrew and Greek — as well as the cultural heritages therein, we broaden our range of experiences with the Spirit and bring awareness to the traditions, practices, and techniques that we are connected to. Many of the descriptions of such practices were lost in the process of the textualization of Scripture and as a result, most spiritual practices preserved within Protestantism[xix] became a form of supplication.

Many people talk about Jewish mysticism or spirituality in the context of meditation, and it is essential to remember that we are dealing with a long history of ideas, practices, methodologies, and techniques both known and lost over a period of three thousand years or so. Within this vast chronological span, we have at least five major ages or periods that contribute to the practices that have been preserved within the Jewish religious context today, especially pertaining to the impacts of meditational and spiritual practices. The first age is that of the Ancient Israelites, which existed before and includes the period of the First Temple, or Solomon's temple (roughly 2000 BCE - 586 BCE). The second age begins with the construction of the Second Temple, its renovations under Herod, and concludes with its destruction, hence the so-called Second Temple period (approximately 516 BCE - 70 CE). The third age is that of the early and middle Rabbinic eras (100 CE - 800 CE); the fourth is the Medieval period (800 CE - 1500 CE) that emerged in Western Europe and north Africa; and the fifth age highlights one of the peaks of Jewish mysticism in Northern Palestine in the 16th and 17th centuries, as well as the Hasidic movement of North-Eastern Europe of the 18th century. Each era carries within itself a mystical tradition or strand that incorporates a variety of techniques and methodologies for accessing Divine realms and altered states.

Where we can safely go back in time and say that various meditational techniques were being used by the Israelites roughly starts around the 8th and

7th centuries BCE. Firstly, based on the biblical texts and corollary historical support, there seem to be prophetic schools during this time that taught the prophets-in-training how to enter into trance-like states in order bring about the "word of the Lord." Secondly, now overlapping into the Second Temple period, the visionary escapades of Isaiah, Ezekiel, and Daniel show that trance states were not only used to evoke a Divine word but also for traversing worlds, dimensions, and realms. What is evidently clear from the texts is that the Israelites and Judaean community were concerned with Divine words pertaining to the nation as a whole and to the collective "We." The majority of prophetic utterances and visionary journeys preserved within the Judaean context were concerned for the people as a whole. We have no preservation of guidebooks or texts that clearly outlined mystical ascent. Instead, we have the prophetic utterances of what apparently emerged from these trance states. It is difficult to say what exactly the ancient Israelites were practicing because most of that information was lost, but there is certainly speculation that some of the techniques or practices were secretly handed down verbally from master to student over the course of many centuries. This, at least at our current point in time, is not demonstrable by any direct evidence and is still in the process of continual discovery and illumination by archaeologists and historians alike.

This next section utilizes a sort of philological archeology through which we can begin to construct a picture of some techniques or practices that were incorporated into the scripture we have today. In the Hebrew Bible, there are three words that are often translated "to meditate:" Hagah (הגה), Siyach (שיח), and Hitbonen (התבונן.)

Firstly, Hagah can also be translated as "to contemplate," or understood as one focusing their mind through speech or noise. For example, "May the words of my mouth, and the meditation (hagayon) of my heart, be acceptable to You, O God" (Psalm 19:15). It can also be seen as a sort of cooing, humming, or rumination of noises or speech that one makes while they are chanting the Divine names, as seen in the following: "In Your Name I lift my hands ... and meditate (hagah) on You in the watches of the night" (Psalm 63:5,6), "I will coo (hagah) like a dove" (Isaiah 38:14), and, "Like a lion and cub growl (hagah) over their prey" (Isaiah 31:4). What we see from Hagah and its use within the Psalms is a sort of mantra-meditation which encourages the reader to focus one's thoughts on the Divine in its attributes and names through speech or sound in order to shift one's awareness that then encourages a continual focus on Spirit.

Furthermore, this word contains the idea of purification or cleansing: "Remove (hagah) the dross from silver ... remove the wicked from before the king" (Proverbs 25:4,5). This purification or cleansing can be akin to the idea that one is bringing their mind to a place of ease and rest so that the Spirit might emerge within. In the process of ruminationing on an attribute or Divine name one begins to clear the dross in their heart-mind which allocates one's awareness to the Spirit. And finally, it is worth noting that this root of Hagah is also related to a similar word meaning "rudder or helm." One can gather from this linguistic relationship that through Hagah-like meditation, or the practice of ruminating and focusing on the aspects of the Divine, one can *steer* the heart so that it no longer wanders aimlessly on the vast sea of the unconscious mind, instead it comes to a watery stillness that reflects the Divine light.

The second example of a word often translated as "to meditate" is Siyach. Siyach-like meditation is the act or process of being mindful, or to be fully aware of the activities of the Divine Spirit. These activities can either be the eventual manifestation of the Divine's works and creations or within the lure of the Divine will. To practice Siyach is to tune one's heart to the activity of the Spirit as it informs it of its work. For example, Psalm 77:13 states, "I meditate (hagah) on all Your works, and in Your plans I meditate (siyach)." And Psalm 119:27 says, "Let me understand the way of Your mysteries, I will meditate (siyach) in Your wonders." As mentioned, Siyach meditation is intended for one to feel for the Divine's gentle persuasion, lure, and movement which contains the Will or ideal vision of the Spirit. To ruminate on these aspects is to ruminate within the domain of the event horizon wherein the Spirit continually flows throughout the open and creative processes of all Worlds. One way this can be simply practiced is to ask the Spirit: what does a harmonious vision of my life look like? After receiving some sort of impression, image, or feeling about this, ruminate on the image and or feeling. Feel it, let it sink in. Focus your mind on the visional reality that the Spirit brought to you for at least for 15 minutes. Don't let it just pass through your system; let it become an aspect that you ponder for many hours.

The third example is Hitbonen, which is often translated as "to look upon," "to understand" or even "to contemplate." The following biblical examples show the range of this word's possibilities:

> "I have made a covenant with my eyes;
> How then could I *gaze* at a virgin?" (Job 31:1)

> "I even *paid close attention* to you;
> Indeed, there was no one who refuted Job..." (Job 32:12)

> "Hear this, O Job; *stop and consider* the wondrous works of God." (Job 37:14)

> "Let those who are wise give heed to these things,
> and *consider* the steadfast love of the Lord." (Psalm 107:43)

> "The wicked lie in wait to destroy me, but I *consider* your decrees.
> I have seen a limit to all perfection, but your commandment is exceedingly broad."

(Psalm 119:95-96)

Each of these passages allude to the practice of directing one's mind to such a degree that understanding begins to emerge through the mind's focus on an aspect of the Divine. This is why Hitbonen is translated as "contemplate" in many translations, for the action of Hitbonen is active and develops the process of actively engaging one's focus upon the nature and actions of the Divine. So in one dimension of its practice it may be viewing a tree and noticing the aesthetic of its beauty and how it reflects hidden realities of Spirit. Or this could even be ruminating on the processual journey of transformation one has had in their life with the Spirit. As we will see in the next section of contemplation, Hitbonen is also cataphatic, that is, an affirmational and often image-based practice wherein one anchors themselves on an image in order to draw oneself into that experience. One way of practicing this method is through imagining and re-imagining a biblical story in your mind over and over again, until a felt or image-based response begins to emerge.[xx]

Similar to the Hitbonen meditation but found within the Christian tradition are the many Orthodox churches who use images or icon-creation in order to meditate and awaken the soul to the Spirit. For those in the Protestant tradition, working without images or centering around an apophatic reality for worship has been their inherited mode of worship since Protestantism's inception in the 16th century. If you have ever been to an Orthodox Church, one the first things you may notice are the various icons or images on the walls. For those that come from a Protestant background, it can be rather startling or even like a form of "idol worship." But for our brothers and sisters in the Orthodox tradition, these icons are viewed as sacred portals for the Divine Spirit, or for even the life of that particular saint or biblical scene, to shine through into the atmosphere of their room or church. These cataphatic traditions hold that such images are transmuting heavenly energies into creation.

An example of what this looks like within such communities is that one may take an icon of Jesus Christ and focus his or her mind on it, that is, watching, feeling, and observing all of the sensations that arise while observing the icon. Because there is such an intense focus on the image, many Orthodox communities recommend that the icon be blessed by a priest before one engages with the image, hence why the artists within these traditions have strict guidelines and certain spiritual protocols to follow. Again, these images are not being worshipped but intended to be utilized as windows with which to engage the Divine *energia* or energy behind them. Other Christian forms of practice will be discussed shortly.

What we have considered thus far in the biblical tradition are actions and practices which draw the meditator toward becoming aware of where the mind is at, what it is focusing on, and where it can be shifted to, as well as the eventual realizations that will ensue. These activities are generally best practiced sitting down or in a position where one can focus their mind upon the life of the Spirit, but this is not the one and only way that one can meditate.

There are also other active types of meditation that occur in the Israelite and Jewish tradition. According to Aryeh Kaplan, a Jewish mystic and author, the "Bible states explicitly that the prophets used chants and music to attain higher states of consciousness."[xxi] He speculates that the Psalms and other musical practices of ancient Israel were not played for simple entertainment but used in order to induce certain states for the listener or practitioner. Kaplan states, "It is significant to note that another word for song, Shir (שיר) is very closely related to the word Shur (שור), meaning 'to see.'"[xxii] He suggests that the words for song and vision are closely related and therefore interconnected in their function toward true mystical visions. This can be exampled in the story of Saul prophesying among the prophets right after he was anointed as king in 1 Samuel 10:5-11:

'After that you shall come to Gibeath-elohim, at the place where the Philistine garrison is; there, as you come to the town, you will meet a band of prophets coming down from the shrine with harp, tambourine, flute, and lyre playing in front of them; they will be in a prophetic frenzy. Then the spirit of YHVH will possess you, and you will be in a prophetic frenzy along with them and be turned into a different person. Now when these signs meet you, do whatever you see fit to do, for God is with you. And you shall go down to Gilgal ahead of me; then I will come down to you to present burnt offerings and offer sacrifices of well-being. Seven days you shall wait, until I come to you and show you what you shall do.' As he turned away to leave Samuel, God gave him another heart; and all these signs were fulfilled that day. When they were going from there to Gibeah, a band of prophets met him; and the spirit of God possessed him, and he fell into a prophetic frenzy along with them. When all who knew him before saw how he prophesied with the prophets, the people said to one another, 'What has come over the son of Kish? Is Saul also among the prophets?'"

Thus, worship, praise, singing, and dancing hold the possibility to shift one's mind into becoming more aware of the Divine Spirit and its flow within. The practitioner, however, must be aware of where their mind is and what it is focusing on during these acts. If you are thinking about lunch while leading worship, it is unlikely that you are entering into the Divine flow, which is enacted through the process of yielding one's mind to the Spirit. The secret ingredient again is found in Psalm 46:10 when it states, "Be still and know that I am God."

As mentioned throughout this guidebook, it does take quite a bit of practice to calm the mind and become solely focused on one's task. Truly, do not be discouraged if you find that your mind is still full of thoughts and scattered, even after six months of practice. Through consistency and patience, you will begin to bring your mind to a place of ease without necessarily trying to halt your thoughts altogether.

As we have seen there were many possible types of meditational practices among the ancient Israelites. They contain different types of intentional focus and processes. What is important to remember is that there *were* different types of meditation occurring among the ancient Israelites that later found their unique expressions in Judaism. If you are looking for a simple place to start, see the practice below that works within a particular practical aspect of the Hagah meditation.

Hagah Meditation Exercise: 10 minutes

Find a name of the Divine that speaks to you or you feel drawn to at the moment. For example, perhaps El Roi, which translates to "the God who sees me." You can do this while sitting quietly or while you are cooking, eating, walking, or doing the dishes. Take the name and repeat it over and over again in your mind. But each time you say it, feel your soul and your body, noticing how your systems respond to the name. This is key — let your heart open in gratitude and love towards the name. Feel it. Let it penetrate every part of you. You can do this for as long as you like.

*"But we all, with unveiled faces, beholding
as in a mirror the glory of the Spirit, are
transforming into that same image from glory
to glory, just as from the life-giving Spirit."*

2 Corinthians 3:18

*"'Teacher, which is the great commandment
in the Law?'*

*And He said to him, 'You shall love the YHVH
your Elohim with all your heart, and with all
your soul, and with all your mind.'*

This is the great and foremost commandment.

*The second is like it, 'You shall love your
neighbor as yourself.'"*

Matthew 22:36-39

5

EARLY CHRISTIAN CONTEXT OF MEDITATION

The early Christian milieu was heavily influenced by Hellenistic culture, including the Stoics, Epicureans and the Platonists, each of whom had ideal practices of contemplation or *theoria*. This *theoria* was not simply a visional activity but one in which the whole of how one lived, behaved, and related to the world and nature became a foundation stone for living out one's contemplative practice. It had to be embodied in order for it to be real.[xxiii] The aspect of contemplation known as *theoria* is mentioned once in the Gospels in Luke 23:48, in which the crucifixion is described as a spectacle (*theoria*). The Gospel's use of this word in this particular scene hints at the idea that the crucifixion of Jesus Christ should be an object of divine gaze that has the capacity to fundamentally transform the way one lives. This scene is to be a pivotal moment for those to take upon the life of Christ within.

Writing in the early first century CE, the Jewish philosopher known as Philo of Alexandria who would go on to influence the Gospel of John with his usage of the Logos, describes all of these activities of the contemplative in their Hellenistic-Jewish community:

> "...thorough investigation (*skepsis*), reading (*anagnosis*), listening (*akroasis*), attention (*prosoche*), self-mastery (*enkrateia*), meditation (*metletai*), practicing indifference to indifferent things, therapies for the passions, remembrance of good things, accomplishment of duties..."[xxiv]

All of these activities were a means for a type of self-realization in which the individual would strive to liberate themselves from their ego in order to bring a type of union with the Good, the One, God, cosmos, or Being itself.[xxv] These activities, as recorded by Philo, were never lost but were incorporated into the practices of the early Church fathers and mothers. They were most notably and intensely implemented in the ascetic practices of the Desert Fathers and Mothers of the fourth century in Syria, Egypt, Turkey, and elsewhere. In addition to Philo's list, these Christian practitioners incorporated a focus on the life of Jesus Christ into their contemplation. These monastics within their contemplative gaze were echoing the words of Paul in 2 Corinthians 3:18:

> "And we, with unveiled faces reflecting like mirrors the brightness of the Divine, all grow brighter as we are turned into that image (*eikon*) that we reflect."

The word "reflecting" used in this verse was translated in the Latin Vulgate as "gazing" or "contemplating." It is to take our focus and to shift it, observing the life of Christ and its process of transforming our very be-ing.

When we begin to adjust our awareness, our sensitivity to the flow the Spirit begins to heighten and our ways of "knowing" begin to change. Once again, one can understand the reasoning for icon gazing through this verse as a form of contemplation as practiced by the Christian Orthodox.

Christian contemplation is not merely a practice of abstraction but one that emphasizes the flow of personal communion. As mentioned previously, the books of Psalms states: "Be still and *know* that I am God." This Yadah (ידע), or process of knowing, is one in which the reader is reminded of coming together in intimate union. This word is used in Genesis to describe the union between Adam and Eve, after which they begat a child. Of course, I am not trying to suggest that sexual union with God is the goal but rather to direct the soul toward the divine union or influx of Spirit that is present within itself. The practice of meditation and contemplation aids the mind and soul to enter into rest, which allows one to sense and acknowledge the realities of union

We must also ask ourselves where our focus lies. Is it on the old human, the old sinful nature that was crucified with Christ? Or are we not now present with the Spirit of Christ that is dwelling within us? With the Spirit as the object of our gaze, we participate in the purification process of one's entire being. 1 John 3:3 states that, "Everyone who has this hope in him, *purifies* himself, just as he is pure." All of these activities participate in the process of *metanoia*, the secret ingredient of embodied transformation according to Romans: "Be transformed, by the renew*ing* (*metanoia*) of your mind"(Rom. 12:2). Repentance is not simply apologizing but is instead the process of shifting one's entire mental activity and position. This cannot be done without focus, discipline, practice and grace. The practice of meditation and mindful attentiveness, re-trains (*metanoia*) the mind in order to restructure or instill within it the "mind of Christ."

In Luke 10, Yeshua explains that one should "Love YHVH your Elohim with all of your heart and with all of your soul and with all of your strength and with all of your mind; and to love your neighbor as yourself." Consider this question: if your mind is constantly distracted and you cannot sit still for more than 10 seconds, how can you even begin to enter into this single-minded, meditational way of living that was prescribed by our Teacher? It is not easy to enter into this devotional reality prescribed by Jesus and that is precisely the point — He wants you to try! And in trying, you begin to observe yourself and to realize that your mind is constantly running, never at peace or ease. It is only after this realization that you can become open to transforming into a vessel of peace. From that moment of acknowledgement and then surrender, you begin to seek the Ecology of the Spirit which will, in time, begin to manifest its presence. There are many fruits of this Ecology that we desire, whether it be power, prophecy, healing, words of knowledge, and other miracles. But we must remember that the call is to seek *first* the Ecology of the Spirit, then all of these things will be added unto us. For when the Ecology begins to emerge within us, these manifestations become a product of the Divine flow that inhabit our life.

As discussed earlier regarding the practices of Jewish communities of which Philo was a part, I encourage you to let all things in your life become a sort of meditation. Attention, learning, investigation, relationships, and reading have all been active parts of my meditational practices that have contributed to my transformations. Believe it or not, I was never the best student growing up. In fact, I barely read at all and probably only read about five books in my adolescence. I simply did not have the attention or discipline to sit down and read. It wasn't until about ten years ago that I started to work on myself spiritually and was able to open this part of myself. Now I can sit and read a few hundred pages a day, but this didn't happen overnight. The focused meditations discussed in this guidebook played a significant role in shifting my neural pathways, allowed for the endurance, and made space for the absorption of large amounts of information and concepts. So, don't restrict what you think meditational practice might entail! Remember the Alexandrian Jewish communities' list above and how the various types of activities contribute to benefiting the whole person.

Seeking Ecology of the Spirit Exercise: 10 minutes

Sit quietly for five minutes. Watch your thoughts. Do not associate with them. After five minutes or when you start to feel yourself come into rest, ask Jesus out loud, "Jesus, what does the Ecology of the Spirit look like? What does it feel like? Guide me on the journey to its discovery." Now relax for a few minutes and set your heart on wanting to know the Ecology of the Spirit. Nothing has to happen in this moment. The intention has been set and you are diving into the realm of silence where the Spirit will in time emerge. If something does occur whether it be a feeling or image, just observe it. After it passes or after a few minutes of sitting, take a deep breath and say "thank you."

"Christ has no body now on earth but yours, no hands but yours, no feet but yours.

Yours are the eyes through which is to look out Christ's compassion to the world;

Yours are the feet with which he is to go about doing;

Yours are the hands with which he is to bless humanity now."

- Saint Teresa of Ávila.

6

INTRODUCING SENSORIUM & THE BODY

The following chapter discusses what I have termed as the "sensorium," which are the faculties that experience the various sensoria or sensations. Just as the nose functions as the faculty for smelling, a sensorium is a center wherein one senses a particular sense. Our ears, eyes, nose, mouth, and skin are all a part of the collective bodily sensorium. When discussing matters pertaining to the sensorium of sensemaking, we must ask ourselves, "What is sensing?" And from there, "What then can be sensed?" It is clear that varied periods of humanity have sensed or related to the world in ways wholly different from how modern, Anglo-Europeans do today. Some have speculated that this may be due to the fact that they were not as evolved or had not developed their minds enough to create the sort of distinctions and abstractions that we possess today. In contrast, I hold to the idea that various cultures in the world of early humanity — and some presently until today, although very few — had certain developed or inherited faculties that facilitated a certain relationship and experience of the world that were entirely different from those of modern societies. Part of the problem, perhaps, of modern humanity is that we tend to think that the majority of humans experienced being human similarly across the board throughout history. Indeed, most of us can acknowledge that there are cultural and environmental differences that develop various mental habitations, but we tend to assume that those differences are due to either a lack of development or the experiencers are merely caught in a web of naïve ignorance. We have forgotten to ask about their underlying perceptions and experiences within the world, and how they made-sense of their lives. What if they *literally* experienced reality differently due to the fact that certain sense faculties were active within their be-ing?

The first place of the sensorium is within the body. Yes, the body! Here we feel, intuit, build, and receive information from the Spirit as it flows through, in, and around us. Too many of us have rejected and ignored our bodies over the years and, as a result, have shut down one of the most incredibly potent vessels for listening and hearing from the Spirit. It is here, from our physical sensorium, that the Spirit, angels, and energies can be felt, seen, and communicated with. Let me put it in very simple terms: your body is an antenna for spiritual energies and activities.

In order to begin to understand the process of the somatic sensorium, one must first analyze and dissect the functionality of sensing-making within our bodies. We must first look at the faculties of sensing since these are the tools or apparatuses by which the process of sensing occurs. These five are the nose, mouth, ears, eyes, and the sense of touch. Of course, these apparatuses are merely a collection of small parts that build each particular "tool," i.e. the irises, pupils, nerves, or pre-frontal, visual cortex. All of these parts collectively build and channel the process of "seeing" within our biological matrix. These parts that collectively build each particular faculty of sensing are all tied to the nervous and limbic system of our bodies that essentially produce the character of the sensed arena of objective reality.

Secondly, in addition to the faculties of our biological sense-making, we have the activity of sens*ing* itself. This is the breath*ing*, feel*ing*, eat*ing*, smell*ing* and touch*ing* processes to which the sense is realized. These are the activities as produced by the tools of our sensing by which the eventual datum of the sensed is realized, or made "real."

Thirdly, we have the informational field of that which is being sensed, or the field of that which contains the quality of that which *will* be sensed. This is, essentially, the objective datum that inhibits the characteristics that the senses will receive. Such qualities are never inherent to the object itself but rather are produced by a plethora of relational processes that in turn create the informational field that will be sensed. We see this in wine making, for example, wherein the taste of a certain wine is produced by a whole host of factors: the minerals in the soil, the types of grape(s), climate, and production methods. All of these relational factors produce the informational field to which our faculties sense.

The fourth aspect is the processual notice or *experience* of that which is being sensed. It is the moment our reality is felt and therefore inundated and shifted by the sense itself. Take for instance the process of tasting. When one is not tasting, he or she is experiencing a reality that contains the quality of barrenness within one's mouth. Usually, the "empty" mouth experience goes unnoticed and our sense of taste is ignored until we put something into our mouths. At the moment we experience the taste of the object that touches our tongue, our experience of reality shifts. We go from tasting to *tasting*. And this latter *tasting* produces a quality of experience that immersively shifts oneself into the very experience itself. To taste or to see or to smell something is to have one's being be infiltrated, shifted, informed, moved, and entirely re-characterized. Sensing itself produces the quality of one's experience from one moment of movement into the next.

Next is the fifth aspect, which is the superjectual process of sensing. After we have sensed the objective datum and have experienced it, we then (usually) project the data of what we have sensed to the object itself. It becomes a looping process in which we are informed by the data while simultaneously projecting the individual experience upon the object itself, thereby giving each object a relatively conditioned response to the field of that which is being sensed. It is within this process wherein values are produced, emotions are created, and perceptions evolve, to only name a few.

Finally, the process by which we communicate our sensed experiences with one another remains the sixth aspect. It is difficult to find an exact replica of experience from one individual to the next because the process by which the sensed data is noticed differs from person to person. For instance, one would think that tasting the same chicken would be nearly identical from person to person, however we know that is experienced as slightly — or drastically —different due to biological, processual, and preferential differences within each person.

All of the above sensing procedures outline the basic production processes of the somatic experience within one's waking state. Such processes can and do shift under altered states, such as in sleep and trance-like experiences, wherein the mind and body traverse new territories. The ways that we interpret and experience our senses within our physical bodies mirror the way in which we sense and interpret the activities of the Spirit. The troubles that many of us have are partly based on the fact that we have ignored our bodies for so long, which shuts down a host of "eyes," or we have yet to activate our specific organs of sensory input. Imagine if you lived your entire life with your nose plugged and never experienced what it was like to smell. In the same way, many of us are walking blindly or have shut down many of our apparatuses that are in communication with the Spirit. In short, do not be afraid to feel — feel, feel feel! It is the foundation of Spiritual insight. Even Yeshua felt the energy leave his body when the woman grabbed onto his garment because he was so in-tuned with his own energy field, knowing that something had left him. He did not accomplish this by seeing, but rather by feeling.

Speaking from personal experience, I use my body all the time to sense and perceive different types of energies around me. I listen to my body as I enter an area for the first time or when I walk into a room. I scan it constantly with my mind for subtle shifts or sensations that I might be feeling, and how they might be communicating to me about something going on around me. I also use my body to feel the Holy Spirit and to tap into the awareness of the presence, since it can be felt physically in our bodies. This process of "feeling" was foreign to me at first but, with practice, has now allowed me awaken my intuitive capacities and to sense the meta-worlds around me. Do not neglect your body — let it become the great vessel for sensing that it was made to be.

When discussing the body, we must first acknowledge the three main centers that are impacted and fine-tuned through meditation for the purpose of feeling, intuiting, and knowing. These three centers are the top of the head (intellectual center), the heart (intuitive-image center), and the stomach (emotional center). Now before discussing the following centers, I must address that the heart is also an emotional center and an intellectual center. The head is also a center for intuiting, and the stomach area is an intellectual and intuiting center as well. It is not that these three centers primarily only work within one parameter — it is simply that these are their primary functions.

In meditation, one may begin to feel their head with their mind. As you are reading this sentence, take a brief moment to stop and feel your head. Do this slowly. With your mind, slowly scan the top, the sides, the back, and the front. Try to feel the inside, and feel the direct center of you brain. Notice the various sensations that arise as you scan. If you do not feel anything, that is okay — just notice that fact and take note. In time, your sensitivity to this area and many areas in your body will begin to arise. Again, take a moment to visualize something. Where do you feel the most tension or twinge of activity as you visualize an image? Take a note of that and continue reading.

Now, feel your heart area — what does it feel like? What are you sensing within this area? What arises in your mind as you focus your attention on that location? Now, let a positive memory come into your mind as you focus on your heart. What does your heart area feel now? Do you have a sense of joy and openness or does it feel cold and closed? If it is the latter, that is okay; now you know where your heart is at. If it is the latter, take a few minutes each day to put your focus on that area and see what comes to your attention. Then speak to your heart and say, "Heart, show me why you are closed. Why are you not feeling? Let us work together to open you back up. Please show me in a dream, or even in a thought, the first thing you want to show me. Thank you, heart." Again, begin to process with your body — it is alive, and it listens!

As for the emotional center in your gut area, take a deep breath and begin to scan that area with your mind. What comes to your attention? What do you feel? This is a powerful area to draw energy from but it can become depleted with the unconscious stress we throw on ourselves everyday. So take a moment to relax and breathe from the belly. Let it know that you will try to be more conscious of the emotions you are carrying in this area. There is a lot one can say about these three centers and their operation and, in fact, it could be another book altogether. But for now, these operative functions are most essential to know. I recommend that you bring attention to these areas often and scan them daily in your daily meditational routines.

Somatic Sensorium Activation: 5 minutes

Sit quietly for two minutes. Breathe easy. After quieting your self for a few more moments, scan your body with your mind. Start with your feet and work your way up, slowly to the top of your head. Notice all of the different tensions or feelings that you have within your body. While you sit there, say gently out loud, "Holy Spirit, show me what it feels like to feel a 'yes' within my body." Observe yourself, notice how you feel, and pay attention if there is any subtle shift that you are now feeling. Now say again gently, "Holy Spirit, show me what it feels like to feel a 'no' within my body." Again observe how you are feeling, notice any subtle shifts, and repeat this process.

Walking Meditation Exercise: 15 minutes

Go outside and go to a place that is surrounded by nature. Take off your shoes. Walk along on the ground. Slowly walk and inhale with one step and exhale with the next. Alternate inhaling and exhaling with your steps. Pay attention to the movement of your body and the way the ground feels beneath your feet. Notice the way your mind and body interact with each other. Become sensitive to their inter-relational process. Let the slow walking calm your mind.

"Let [the contemplative practice] do
the working, and you be the material
it works upon; just watch it, and let
it be . . . you simply be the wood, and
let it be the carpenter."

- *The Cloud of Unknowing*

7

THE BEGINNINGS OF MIND(FULL) LIVING AND CENTERING PRAYER

As you begin to become aware of the various sensoriums within the Soul and Body as related to Spirit, perhaps one of the first aspects you will notice are the various activities taking place within your mind. This is an aspect of conscious living in Christ that one needs to address: the arena of the collective-heart field. This field is the place that one needs to cultivate awareness of so that one can plant the proper seeds into one's be-ing. Within this collective-heart field, one plants the seeds of their own thoughts among those learned from our parents, society, media, ancestors, schooling, friends, colleagues, and beyond. By practicing awareness in this regard, it helps one to identify those seeds within one's being that need to be further nurtured in order to truly aid one's be-ing. Over time, as we learn to mature the proper seeds of our be-ing, a transformation takes place in every arena of self-production.

How we cultivate these seeds determines the quality or nature of the experiences of one's be-ing. It does not mean that one will not undergo trials or sufferings but rather that the seeds sprout or show their true quality when these events occur. The more we transmute our bitterness, anger, resentfulness, attachments, hatred, and unforgiveness into seeds of freedom, joy, gratitude, and equanimity, the more our be-ing will exude the heavenly Ecology of the Spirit. The Ecology of the Spirit is an accessible reality to all in each and every moment, and it only takes a simple adjustment of one's mind to focus on one of these life giving seeds or an aspect of Divine presence. The seed of this Ecology is present within us by way of the mind of Christ, which exists within oneself as the anointed aspect of consciousness that is fully loving, free, and self-giving. Although it is freely accessible, it must be realized, cultivated, and brought to a place of awareness so that the aspects of its activity might become actualized.

One might think of this heart-field as the place where one draws their thoughts *from* and where one draws their thoughts *to*. If one is constantly thinking negatively or is imagining horrible things being done to another out of anger and hatred, it seeds into the heart-field a sort of quality of actuality that in time can cause one to act upon what they are constantly sowing. It is for this reason that the second letter to the Corinthians 10:5 states, "We are destroying speculations and every lofty thing raised up against the knowledge of God, and we are taking every thought *captive* to the obedience of Christ." But the first step, as we have been discussing, is to become aware of what you are thinking, to become aware of the emotions that you are carrying. For it is only when you begin to observe yourself that you have the power to shift your mind into a conscious moment of communion with the mind of Christ. Try to watch and observe what you are thinking, saying, and doing. When you are in such meditational practices, observe, feel, intuit, and above all, do not be afraid of what you might find within. Some of it may be the fruit of some bad seeds, but that is okay! The life of the Divine Presence and the Ecology of the Spirit is ever deeper still, and its light will soon shine as you bring your awareness within.

Other ways that one may become aware of their thoughts are through traditional, Christian spiritual practices, such as centering prayer. Centering prayer resurfaced in the 1970s and has gained popularity within certain streams of Christianity over the last decades. If this path interests you and you would like to know more about this practice, I recommend Cynthia Bourgeault's wonderful book entitled, *Centering Prayer and Inner Awakening*. Put simply, the practice of centering prayer revolves around a time of sitting with mindful attention to our thoughts and the spaces between them. The practitioners constantly bring their awareness back to restful place of watching. One is advised never to associate with one's thoughts or to follow them but to merely watch them flow by. Through the act returning to the awareness of watching or observing, one is "centering" themselves and allowing the Spirit to communicate. Over time from this watchful place, the Spirit begins to emerge through the restful state of observance.

Centering Prayer Exercise: 20 minutes

Find a place to sit quietly for about fifteen minutes. Make sure you are sitting up straight with your feet flat on the ground. Gently bring your attention to your thoughts and mind. Notice what you are thinking about. Notice that your mind is likely running and thinking, as it is most the time. Don't associate yourself with the thoughts. Simply sit back and watch them stream by. If you find yourself being carried away by your thoughts, simply bring yourself back to the awareness that you are just watching them. Scan your body, pay attention to how you are feeling, again do not associate with any feeling. Just observe and return to the "watcher" watching and feeling.

"*I know of no other Christianity and of no other Gospel than the liberty both of body and mind to exercise the Divine Arts of Imagination.*

I rest not from my great task! To open the Eternal Worlds, to open the immortal Eyes of Humanity. Inwards into the Worlds of Thought; Into eternity, ever expanding. In the Bosom of God, The Human Imagination."

- *William Blake*

8

THE IMAGE SENSORIUM

The insights on the image sensorium and its functions discussed in this chapter have emerged from a ten-year process of daily engagement. Its processes and usages are essential for all different types of emotional, spiritual, and intellectual work that I use on a day-to-day basis. It is vitally important that this sensorium is awakened and brought into conscious understanding if one wants to engage in deeper aspects of meditation.

What many call the imagination, I call the image sensorium, which has two primary functions: the imaginal and the visional. Any activity within the heart-mind that is a built or consciously constructed image is an activity of the imaginal, by way of the heart center. In contrast, any activity that is passively experienced or revealed is of the visional. These two functions do, of course, blend together and form the processes that serve as vehicles for transpersonal communication. It is the arena of the mind that allows for meta-noetic transference of information, both personal and cosmic in sensations and images. The image sensorium is not only what one does with their heart-mind, but is also the very place from which one draws inspiration, communication, transference, transcendence, (in)scendence, vision, information, revelation, and creation. It is the great receptor of the realms of the heavenly worlds.

Often times, those who use terminology about "ascension" or "stepping into heaven" or any sort of terminology used when discussing mystical practice are usually referring to methodologies that require the use of creative mental image-making within the heart-mind. What many are activating while performing these activities is the *imaginal*, since it is the process by which one inscribes an image or world upon their heart-mind in order to access certain archetypal manifestations of the collective mind or Spirit. For example, when one says, "Go visit a garden" and he or she gives you the details of its imagery, this utilizes the imaginal aspects of our creative heart-mind as it creates through archetypal information. The benefits of the imaginal are easy to acquire when one mixes a passive openness with it, or with the visional, in order for revelatory information to flow. If one knows how to do this then this activity becomes beneficial in a number of arenas of one's life:

1. Provides conscious access to the mind of the Divine

2. Creates a space for the Spirit of Jesus Christ to come into relational activities of the Soul

3. Opens the door of opportunity for angelic relationships

The difficulty with using imaginal processes alone is that one may come to think that they are actually in *the* heaven, when in reality they are in a self-created world that is flowing with the Divine presence from within themselves. In a sense, this world is adding to the nested dimensional possibilities of the heavens, but the collective familial world that we call "heaven" is not a self-created space. It is rather a world that one flows into through the openness to the Divine Spirit. Access to it is only realized through surrender or through ecstatic elevations on the contemplation of the Divine Presence. I am in no way against one creating these inner spaces. In fact, they are vitally important because they act as informational spaces that one interacts with and also observes. For instance, the imaginal can be used as a house of discernment because it provides an arena for trans-world data to manifest to one's conscious mind. In the process of structuring an imaginal world, one is invited into the mysterious depths of one's own be-ing, both real and in potential.

Furthermore, the imaginal is a gateway to profound realizations, healing, insight and communication. One way to have some of these profound benefits emerge is for one to surrender his or her own heart-mind to the Spirit after entering these spaces. Let us say that one is talking with Jesus in the imaginal, that is, you are self-creating an image of Jesus in your image sensorium. In order for revelatory informational to flow, one must pair the imaginal with passive moments of connection. In other words, one must learn to suspend the self-generated, active heart-mind so that one can bypass the conscious mind and the ego to whatever extent it can. This allows the words or information being received to go beyond insular "self-talk" and instead opens the possibility for the Divine mind to communicate and reveal through the use of imaginal workings. This requires one to have situated their heart-mind in a restful place, to have surrendered the heart-mind to be open to receive the words that are spontaneously generated within the heart-mind through the Spirit. Again, the essential key here is to begin to center oneself, to quiet the mind, and to gently open one's heart so that the Spirit can be sensed.

The imaginal is central and one of the most utilized techniques by many in new Christian mystical movements, however, many often lack understanding as to what is occurring in their practices. Many of these movements believe that the process of "stepping into heaven" is a form of heavenly ascension and in some ways it can be since the faith generated within that moment does unleash the activity and presence of the Spirit. However, if one wants to *solely* work from the place of the imaginal, then I recommend that one should spend many hours of intentional focus with their imagery because when an image is held in the mind's eye or is engraved within the image sensorium for long periods of time, inspiration, revelation, transformation, begin to emerge. The transference can become so intense that a real bond or relationship may arise and the reality of that world may manifest within the realm of one's awareness.

When we actively imagine the Ecology of the Heavens in the image-sensorium, we are awakening the innate, harmonic human possibility that lies dormant within the fabric of the eros of Spirit. Such activities transverse the individual into archetypal cosmic landscapes that are inhabited by one's own personal matrix of characters, both self-created and transpersonal, such as angels, cloud of witnesses, and so on. Such characters can use the image sensorium for communication and transformation. Additionally, these self created worlds may function like a dream-world in that they can be instantaneously destroyed by one's own will just as quickly as they were created. This is part of the beauty and power of the capabilities of the image sensorium.

There are also times when one should tear down and rebuild their inner worlds according to the inspirational guidance of the Holy Spirit. It is within this dance of the spirit that one enhances the scope of each worldly creation. In their creation and its deconstruction, back into the waters of potential, such assimilation and dissimulation processes allow the Spirit to bring an ever-intensified realization of and union with its life, love, activity, and revelation.

Should one use the imaginal tool with caution? Of course, as is the case with any spiritual tool. It is with this tool that one can easily become caught in delusion or fantasy, which are nothing but imagery completely drawn from egoic and self-centered interests. They do not seek inspiration from beyond oneself and occur when one misrepresents the process or the world that one sees. If it is a self-created world then one needs to simply realize that it is a *self*-created world. If it is a self-created world that seeks its own transformation, then that is just that. Fantasy occurs when one embellishes, mischaracterizes, or uses what one sees or creates for egoic power gains. Fantasy can also occur out of our needs, i.e. sexual, professional, or even spiritual. As for delusion, it is difficult to say what is delusional since each person carries within themselves a partial view unless their mind is fully clear. What is important is how we characterize the information. Fantasy usually fulfills self-centered desires and flourishes when one seeks their own praise. But it isn't exclusively negative since it has the potential to reveal areas in which one feels unloved or devalued, which offer an opportunity for awareness and integration. It can also show itself as an unconscious place to mentally pacify needs, which can be driven by trauma or a lack of clarity of the Presence. Furthermore, it can be a type of self-communication or self-reflective space wherein one gets a glimpse of their mental and emotional needs. Sometimes once can consciously draw oneself into fantasy in order to build up confidence or to see the areas that one's negative tendencies need to be addressed. One can also enter this space in order to hold up a hopeful and declarative vision of one's victorious life without it being purely fantastical.

The most efficient way to "ascend," "(in)scend," or move into non-self created worlds is to enter into visional activity. The visional is the process in which one sits back and watches the mind unfold. When most people close their eyes, they will see nothing but darkness or maybe some patches of color here and there. They then often become restless and start to create images in their head, like a library or a great city, and then go explore. Again, that is absolutely fine, but one must be aware that they are entering into an archetypal informational center, which certainly has the capacity to flow with Divine presence. To sit and wait or to stir the mind by ecstatic, focused worship, in contrast, is not easy right away. It requires focus, discipline, and willingness to push through. What does occur, however, when one finally breaks through the threshold are vistas and worlds beyond imagination that begin to flood into the mind's inner eye. In those moments, one only needs to step back, relax, and watch. It can be difficult to not want to jump in and divert the process with your own will, although there are times it opens up to that. I recommend, however, that when this does occur one should sit back and let the visionary experience unfold. The passive visional or the model of "be-ing still" is one of the most difficult things for Westerners to practice. In my own practice, I found it extremely difficult at the beginning and it took me many years to come to enjoy. But if you can shift yourself to not "jump the gun," the ascension process by way of the Spirit will open itself to you in profoundly novel ways.

The other thing I might warn against is an attachment to extra-ordinary experiences. One of the tendencies I have observed within new Christian mystical movements is that many expect to have exceptional and extraordinary experiences every time they go to sit down. What this unrealistic expectation produces is impatience and disappointment when the passive images fail to flood in. There are many days I go to sit down for a few hours and little to nothing incredible happens during that time. But in the *process* and the *practice* itself, I am shifting and balancing my emotions and heart, and walk away totally refreshed from be-ing in the Presence. If you are able to understand this part of the journey early on, you will save yourself from the burden of disappointment and the desire to quit. The experiences will come, I assure you. And if you are patient and fall in love with the process, truly enjoying sitting in the restful presence of Spirit, you will be shown things beyond anything you could have ever put into words. This means, of course, that one must be acquainted with the experience of silence. One of my favorite Christian monastics and a true master in the meditative lifestyle is St. Isaac, a Syrian Christian monk from the 7th century. He composed the following beautiful homilies on silence:

> "What watering is to plants is exactly the same as continual silence for the growth of spiritual knowledge."
>
> "Silence is a mystery of the age to come, but words are instruments of this world."
>
> "True wisdom is gazing at God. Gazing at God is silence of the thoughts."[xxvi]

In order to step into the visional, one must be open to the activity of the stillness of silence. As one begins to dive into the mysterious depths of the ever-unfolding presence of the Divine, one will notice that the deeper one goes, the more silent one becomes. Silence is not a characteristic of unconscious behavior but a resting into the nature of one's union with Christ. It is seen in the calming and stilling of one's mind. It is seen in the openness of one's heart towards the work of the Spirit. It is seen in self-less acts of restorative actions. When you begin to enter into silence, let it guide you into the depths of your soul wherein the Fountain of Life springs. It is here where one begins to gaze upon the beatific light of the unfading Presence of the Spirit. Do not be afraid of silence or resist its arising but rather welcome its calming touch to expand your awareness. Here the visional begins to emerge, reminding us again to not become attached to what we experience. The more you open yourself to the Spirit and passively watch, the longer and more intense the visional activities within the image sensorium can take place.

Turning to meditational practices, what do they do for oneself regarding the visional and the imaginal activities?

- Allows for visional reception to become intensified

- With time and focus dedicated to image creation, it can become intensified

- Allows one to feel and recognize what type of image is "incoming"

- Aids the in the development of "sensing"

- Creates the awareness of the tool, or eye, that senses its opening or closing in order to understand what type of image is presented

- Creates a sensitivity to oneself that brings awareness to when the "self" is generating a moment when we are seeking revelation

- Develops the sensitivity for discernment, which can become quick like a reflex over time, because it uses feeling as its primary conduit

- Brings an awareness of our subtle bodies and their activities, which allows us to use the imagination as a tool to navigate those spheres and to influence their actions

- Draws us to silence in order to create the vessel for transformation and possibility within imaginative practices

- Allows us to wake up, be honest, and to see ourselves clearly, which in turn allows us to better see the Spirit. As Yeshua said, "Blessed are the pure in heart for they shall see God" (Mat. 5:8).

In summary, what is the center for the image-sensorium?

1. The center for image creation (imaginal) and image reception (visional)

2. A communication device:

- A faculty for knowing

- A faculty for transforming

- A faculty for creating

- A faculty for awakening

The key in engaging the image-sensorium is allowing yourself space to know when you are projecting or self-creating the imagery. Again, self-creating is not necessarily a negative or positive activity of the image sensorium. Both the imaginal and visional have their own functions and work hand in hand. For instance, when creating for a purpose or looking to create a connection, use the imaginal. When seeking information, on the other hand, try using the visional or the imaginal with the visional's passivity.

To conclude, it is important to note that these are not wholly separate functionalities. They are always present and working together within the image sensorium. If you are seeking an encounter with Jesus, and have used an imaginal process in order to create an image of his form in your image sensorium, the next step is to halt the projection of your thoughts onto Him and instead begin the listening process by passively entering into silence, or the visional, and allowing the Spirit to speak. This takes time and practice but really is the key to having the imaginal come alive and become something that can circumnavigate the ego. Meditation has the potential to tune our perception and awareness to become conscious of when these certain processes are taking place within us. It allows us to finely tune this apparatus to allow the Holy Spirit to give us a vision of the world re-enchanted with the ever-living presence of the Divine.

Imaginal Exercise: 15 minutes

Sit or lie down, making sure you stay awake and are sitting up straight or that your back is flat on the ground. This is to ensure that the energy flow is not restricted within your body. Take a few deep breaths and begin to relax your body. After doing this a few times, take a deep breath and imagine light coming into your heart. Again, after a few breaths of breathing in light within your heart, imagine that Jesus is seated in the center of your heart. He is radiant, full of light and love. With each breath, Jesus becomes brighter and brighter and His light begins to expand. Let your body feel the expansion of the light within your heart. Notice how your mind is interacting with it. Keep breathing until the light begins to overflow into and throughout your entire body, every cell. There is no need to strive, just let it flow and expand. You are now present with the His light. Pause and rest.

"But what now is the meaning of Moses' entry into the darkness and of the vision of the Divine that he enjoyed in it?….But as the soul makes progress, and by a greater and more perfect concentration comes to appreciate what the knowledge of truth is, the more it approaches this vision, and so much the more does it see the divine nature is invisible. It thus leaves all surface level appearances not only those that can be grasped by the senses but all those that the mind itself seems to see, and it keeps on going deeper until by the operation of the Spirit it penetrates the invisible and incomprehensible, and it is there it sees the Divine."

- Gregory of Nyssa, Life of Moses

9

APOPHATIC EC-STASIS

Another Christian meditational practice is one that is centered around apophatic engagement. *Apophasis* is the Greek word for saying "no" or by adhering to a type of negation. There are two prominent Christian mystics, amongst others, who used this technique in order to ascend or (in)scend into the depths of the Spirit. In the late fifth and early sixth centuries CE, Psuedo-Dionysius the Areopagite was the first to popularize and bring attention to this technique and process for Christian mystical engagement, which later influenced many of the greatest mystics and theologians within the Church.[xxvii] The second major contributor to this type of mystical meditative engagement was the anonymous author of the medieval text *The Cloud of Unknowing*. As stated within my introduction, I will not be unraveling all of the various implications of these mystical texts and approaches within this book. But for those who are interested in exploring these approaches, I recommend starting with *The Cloud of Unknowing* and the magnificent mystical works of Pseudo-Dionysius, Meister Eckhart and Saint Gregory of Nyssa.

For me, this practice felt quite foreign the first few times I engaged with it. At times, it even felt sacrilegious and scandalous! But with persistence I began to witness various breakthroughs in the ways I had related to the Divine. Old, unhealthy conceptualizations quickly began to fade away regarding how I had thought about the Spirit. What became apparent to me through this technique were the ways I had constructed my image of the Divine with my own heart. Through the radical deconstruction process of the apophatic way, I was able to open up new possibilities and conceptualties of the Spirit that now enable me to not only relate to the Divine in healthier capacities but dismantle underlying, constrictive thought processes. As a result, my heart-mind was able to expand in ways I did not know were possible.

The apophatic method operates in such a way that it negates all types of images and characteristics that one may attach to the Divine.[xxviii] The following excerpt from *The Cloud of Unknowing* showcases what this process looks like during contemplative practices:

> "And if any thought rises up and keeps on wanting to force itself
> above you, between you and that darkness, and asks you, 'What
> are you seeking, and what would you have?', say that it is God
> you would have: 'I want him, I seek him, and nothing but him.'
> And if it asks you what that God is, say that it is God who made
> and redeemed you, and who has graciously called you to his love;
> and say that you have no understanding of him. And therefore
> say, 'Get back down', and tread the thought down firmly with a
> stirring of love, even though it seems to you most holy, and as
> though it would help you to seek God."[xxix]

The process described is based on negation or denying the various aspects one has attributed to the Divine. It is not wholly expressed in a way so as to remove the Divine's existence from our thoughts but to remind ourselves that we never have a perfectly clear picture of the Spirit. In the excerpt below, medieval mystic and contemporary to the author of *The Cloud*, St. Denis explains his understanding of apophasis as detailed in *The Cloud of Unknowing*:

"And then, ascending and beginning our denials and negations at the highest of intelligible things, we say that he is neither soul nor angel, nor does he have imagination or opinion or reason or understanding; nor is he reason or understanding; nor is he spoken or understood. And – to pass from these high things by intermediate stages to the lowest things – he is not number, or order, or greatness, or littleness, or equality, or likeness, or unlikeness; nor does he stand or move or keep silence or speak. And – to turn back by intermediate stages to the highest things, and end our denials at the highest – we say that he has no power, nor is he power, or light, nor does he live, nor is he life or substance or age or time, nor is there any intelligible contact with him, nor is he knowledge or truth or kingship or wisdom or one or unity or Godhead or goodness; nor is he spirit according to our understanding of spirit; nor sonship nor fatherhood nor anything else known to us or to any who exist; nor is he any of the things that do not exist or any of the things that do exist; nor does any of the things that are known know him as he is; nor does he know the things that exist as they are in themselves, but as they are in him; nor is there any means of approaching him by reason or understanding; he has no name; there is no knowledge of him; he is neither darkness nor light, neither error nor truth; nor, all told, can he be affirmed or denied, but when we attribute by affirmation or remove by denial any or all of the things that are not himself, we can neither posit nor negate him, nor in any intelligible way affirm or deny him. For the perfect and unique Cause of all things must necessarily lack the possibility of comparison with the highest height, and be above all positing and negation. And his incomprehensible transcendence is incomprehensibly above all affirmation and denial."ˣˣˣ

In the excerpt above, one can see a clear negation of a number of attributes that are often assigned to the Divine. And there is nothing wrong with that — this is a contemplative exercise! For the person who has never done this sort of process of negating all attributes one has attributed to the Divine, this can be seen as rather extreme, abrasive, or nerve wrecking. This approach is not to deny the existence of the Divine but to recognize that one's *idea* of the Divine — whether it be of love, wisdom, or knowledge — is nowhere near the actuality of it in regards to the way it is known by the Divine. It is through this detachment of one's ideas of the Divine that one can then be given an intensified realization of the Divine that superseded their previous conceptions. It allows one to be constantly in flow and in process with how one might perceive the Divine so as to not get it caught in a static conception or "idol." The negation creates a womb-like space wherein the Spirit can come and reveal in an intensified way that would have shattered one's previous conceptions. For some, a practice like this can feel shaky, watery, and chaotic, but letting go of one's conceptions of the Divine for a moment (remember, it is not forever — it is done in intentional practice) can allow the Spirit to engender an open vessel for transformation that allows for new creative possibilities to emerge.

A Beginner's Apophatic Exercise Meditation: 10 minutes

Sit quietly for a moment and take a few deep breaths. Bring to your awareness an image of Yeshua. Say gently out loud, "Yeshua, I let go all of the pre-conceived ideas of what you look like physically. Lead me to your nature in Spirit." Feel, breathe, and look within. If anything arises, say "I know you are not wholly that," let it go, and gently say "Show me more." After sitting for ten minutes of letting things arise and fall away, think of an image of Yeshua in your mind and say, "Thank you for showing me that you are so much more than anything I could imagine or conceive."

"The Divine beneath you,

The Divine in front of you,

The Divine below you,

The Divine above you,

The Divine within you."

- Saint Patrick

10

BE-ING PRESENT WITH THE PRESENCE

Part of what is missing within Christian practice is the recognition of the moment or of the "now." This term, of course, has found its way into popular culture and become somewhat of a universal mantra, but it is still a truth that, when focused on, becomes a gateway into truly awakening to one's be-ing. It reinvigorates the soul and reconnects one to the realization that one is existing. It puts one into the space of becoming consciously aware that they are alive, breathing, thinking, and moving. To be gently reminded of this fact allows oneself to reterritorize their current state, or rebalance one's inner territory. This reterritorzation is a "waking up" that moves one into the simple self-recognition of one's existence, beauty, fragility, and strength. To exist is awe-some. It evokes an infinite number of questions, self-reflections, and moments of unutterable existence. And it is this reflection, this simple notice, that opens the door to the influx of Divine presence. For it is in this moment of "now" that flows thought us like a river that the Divine exists, permeates, and intoxicates our activity of be-ing. It invites us into to the Ecology of the Spirit, which moves and enacts within the presence of the unfolding of the moment. I must add that the moment we experience as "now" isn't truly the "now" but a simple momentary reflection of a moment that has swiftly passed by. We do not live in the atomization of time but in an ever-perpetual flow that is presently moving within the ever-unfolding, continual moments we experience as "now."

One of the easiest ways to increase the amount of time that one is alive is to practice being present in the moment. If we live our daily lives constantly in auto-pilot or within our minds, whether it be in the past or the future, we do not get the benefit of being present within the moment. Instead, we are living our lives similar to that which we experience in a dream. If we live like this, we never truly become real. This causes us to be caught in automations of our minds which never allow us to be present and open to the moments we live. To be alive is to first recognize that one is alive, followed by becoming aware of that moment's reality. To be in touch with that living presence in the moment is to finally begin to wake up: "Awake, oh sleeper, and arise from your sleep." Becoming present allows oneself to get in touch with one's body, emotions, the Spirit, and the flow of life. It brings the mind back to the real and out of fantasy land. To bring the mind back to the present moment is not an easy task, but if one can take the time to reel it back in, the benefits will soon emerge as one returns as Soul in communion with the Spirit.

Throughout our days, we participate in a host of activities, some of which we cannot help but be a part of. Only a few are called to be monks and nuns. So then, what are we to do with all of these activities in our lives? We are to participate in be-ing, not doing. If you take a moment in your activity to realize that you are there, present and alive, you will begin to awaken from auto-pilot. As an example, let us say you are cooking. Take a moment to feel the wooden spoon. Notice how it feels in your hand and really look at its colors. Pay attention to all of the details of the vegetables you are cutting. Really notice the different amounts of pressure it takes to cut through each type. Take a moment to smell, to truly smell, what you are cooking. Notice every type of scent that arises through the aroma. If your kids are running around, notice the moment, that it will not be like this forever. But in this moment, their voices, the footsteps, the smells — they are all there, fully present. Many of you might be saying, "Yes yes! I have done this! I have had moments like this in my life that I said 'I will always remember this moment.'" That is indeed the moment you started to awaken from auto-pilot and truly became present in the moment. In fact, most of our memories are moments where we were fully present. The truth is that we can live presently like we do in these fleeting moments, reawakening again and again.

In daily life, we have tasks, chores, people to visit, noise, work, commuting, and entertainment that grab our attention, energy, and presence. None of these are inherently bad, but simply a condition of our world at this time and a part of the song and dance of our incarnation in this age. All of the busyness makes it tough for one to get into the flow of slowing down, becoming still, and opening oneself up to the Spirit. Because of this, our minds are constantly racing and we rarely take a breath to simply be present and open to the moment we live in. It can be hard to stop, look up at the sky, open our hearts to gratitude, and become still for only a moment. All of these difficulties aside, if we can start developing an inner alarm clock or a bell to wake us up to the moment a few times a day —figuratively or literally— we begin to deepen our sense of in-touch-ness with ourselves, the earth, our heart, our families, and the Spirit.

As we have returned to many times throughout this guidebook, the book of Psalms highlights this reality in its statement, "Be still and know that I am God" (Psalm 46:10). Through our practice of stillness and the shifting of our focus to the presence of the Spirit which is always present in the here and now, we begin to reconfigure our awareness and gaze upon the Divine. Over time, this reconfiguration begins to restructure our thought patterns, behaviors, emotions, and overall view of the world. What better time to re-awaken our sense of connection with the world and the gift of life we have all been given than now?

It is important to note that our movement towards the presence in the present will not always be easy or even take us towards positive emotions. We may feel deep pain or anguish, or experience the need for cathartic crying. It can be tough for many individuals, especially if they have buried so many of their emotions within in order to survive, or out of fear and the desire to avoid all types of pain. But when one is present, one is confronted with the fears, pains, and all of the things one has swept under the rug. It can be overwhelming, to be sure, but I promise that in a short amount of time through meditation, contemplation, and consciously present worship one can begin to heal and move into a place of wholeness that echoes the deepest places of inner love while we carry our bumps, bruises, and scars. These painful scars should not be seen as shameful but recognized as markers or areas of deliverance in our journey. One way to shift ourselves into wholeness or into a place of healing is through being mindfully present with the Presence.

One can say that by being present, one is within their True Self (Be-ing) and may enter into wholeness. But let us ask, what exactly is wholeness? Many think that wholeness is utter perfection, a state that carries with it no "flaws" or imperfections. But wholeness is actually (w)holisitic and it carries within it the entire journey, the brokenness and healing, the imperfection and perfection, the reminder of where we came from and where we are headed. Some might ask, "Well, doesn't it all go away? I don't want to remember where I came from." But be reminded, even after Jesus resurrected from the dead, he still carried upon and within his body the markers of his crucifixion. The holes were still present within his flesh. His body reflected his whole journey. It is our imperfections through our journeys, stories, and processes that make us unique, inspiring, beautiful, and miraculous.

I cannot emphasize enough the importance of practicing self-reflection or realization and the process of reminding ourselves that we are present with the Presence. Without this practice, it is unlikely that I would have been able to continually move forward and progress with my spiritual practices. It causes me to be continually honest with myself. It is not always easy, of course, because there are times I sense nothing but pain or a sense of the void. But in time, that openness births something truly new within. Thus, as you draw into the present moment, open your heart, let it heal, let yourself feel, and know that the Spirit is shifting, healing, and restoring your entire be-ing.

Present with the Presence Sitting Meditation: 20 minutes

There are a number of different methods and ways one can enter into the practice of meditation. To begin one must seek out a comfortable location, a chair, couch or cushion. The main goal is to have your back straight whether you are sitting in a chair or lying down. After you have done this, you may begin with taking a few deep inhales. You might notice that your mind is running and racing — that is okay and normal for anyone coming into the practice of meditation. The goal is not to try to stop the thoughts but to pause, observe, and watch as your thoughts go by. Notice what you are thinking about: is it necessary in that moment? After a minute of sitting quietly take a couple of deep inhales again. Finally, gently say over yourself "Jesus Christ" while filling your heart with gratitude for twenty minutes. Notice how your body feels as you say the name, paying attention to the small changes that might be taking place in your system. Remember the goal of meditation is not to fall asleep but to become more perceptive, sensitive, and aware. It is to still one's waters so that one can enter into the transformative processes and place of communication.

"You know that our breathing is the inhaling and exhaling of air. The organ that serves for this is the lungs that lie around the heart, so that the air passing through them thereby envelops the heart. Thus breathing is a natural way to the heart. And so, having collected your mind within you, lead it to the channel of breathing through which air reaches the heart and, together with this inhaled air, force your mind to descend into the heart and to remain there...when you thus enter into the place of the heart, as I have shown you, give thanks to the Divine and, praising Its mercy, keep always to this doing, and it will teach you things that in no other way you will ever learn."

- Nicephorus the Solitary

11

BREATH

"This is the account of the heavens and the earth when they were created, in the day that the YHVH Elohim made earth and heaven. Now no shrub of the field was yet in the earth, and no plant of the field had yet sprouted, for the YHVH Elohim had not sent rain upon the earth, and there was no human to cultivate the ground. But a mist used to rise from the earth and water the whole surface of the ground. Then the YHVH Elohim formed the human of dust from the ground, and breathed into his nostrils the breath of life; and the human became a living being (*nefesh chaya*)." Genesis 2:4-7

Throughout the exercises in this book, you may have noticed that the breath plays a prominent role in calming the body and mind while shifting one's awareness to the activity of the the Spirit. In the Biblical narrative of the creation account of humanity in Genesis 2, it says that the Divine breathed into the first human the breath of life, thereby making it a living soul. Within the narrative, the human was not alive until the breath of the Divine entered into his body. Breath or air is seen within this account as one of the life-forces, something that animates and gives life to the human body. Put simply, one would die without breath. Similarly, just as air gives life to bodies, so does the Spirit give life to souls. It allows us to have a conscious experience of existing. Without Spirit or a fundamental awareness, we would be floating in a world of potentialities. The Spirit, just like the breath, is what makes one actual.

Within our body we have more than one type of wind or breath. We have, of course, the air that flows in and out of our lungs, and we also have the flow of blood that is circulating throughout our system. Finally, we have the flowing energetic fields that move through our nervous system. All of these are a type of wind or breath. Each moves and gives life to our body, and without any of these three activities one would no longer be alive. So, as you go deeper into meditation, make a point of becoming more acquainted with your breath. Notice how the primary intake nostril shifts every couple hours or so. Notice what breathing fast does to your heart, or breathing slowly. Our mind, brain, and bodies shift through our rhythms of breath and through the alterations of our breath, we can shift our perceptions of reality as well as our sensitivity to the Spirit.

The breath has been a major key for me in unlocking the ability to concentrate. When I first started my meditational journey, I would sit down and would try to clear my mind. After a few minutes I would get bored, my mind would wander, and I would quickly get lost in my thoughts. After a short while, however, I found that focusing on the breath allowed my mind to engage and focus on something while I was sitting. Getting to know the breath and truly paying attention to its nuances eased my mind, which allowed for restful states to emerge. For me, the breath has opened up flow states that have allowed for greater clarity in spiritual reception and heartfelt engagement with the Spirit. Through a simple concentration of the breath at night, I have left my body many times. Although it is may seem like an extremely basic concept, it is incredibly powerful. I must note here that there are many, many ways to engage the breath that are foundational for a variety of spiritual engagements, such as bodily attunement and to unlock meta-states of consciousness. The simple exercise below is an excellent place to start and is both foundational and powerful.

Breathing Meditation: 15 minutes

Find a place to sit quietly and upright. Now pray gently out loud, "Holy Spirit, may I become aware of you in the breath." Now take a few deep breaths. Breathe in easily and calmly through the nose. Breathe in for four seconds, hold for four seconds, then breathe out for four seconds. While you are breathing, focus all of your attention on the breath. Notice how the air moves in and out of your nose. What does it smell like? Do you smell anything? Notice the temperature of the air as it enters your nose and notice how it changes as you exhale. Bring your awareness to the breath as you inhale and exhale. If your mind wanders, simply bring your attention back to the breath. Let the breathe calm, massage, and soothe your body. Let your mind slowly come into a place of peace and ease.

"No creature has meaning without the Word of the Divine.

The Divine's Word is in all creation, visible and invisible.

The Word is living, being, spirit, all verdant greening, all creativity.

This Word flashes out in every creature.

This is how the Spirit is in the flesh - the Word is indivisible from the Divine."

- Hildegard of Bingen

12

CLOSING THOUGHTS

Throughout the course of this book, you have encountered various forms and techniques to awaken yourself to the flow of the Spirit within. If you begin to practice the basic tenets of self-observation and quieting your mind, it will open wide the door for conscious participation with the Spirit. There are, of course, many other techniques and ways that one can meditate that this guidebook did not discuss. But by patiently practicing the exercises at the end of each section, one may begin to see the Ecology of the Spirit within oneself. The Holy Spirit moves, flows, and is constantly speaking to us in the silence of our be-ing. The difficult task at hand is to create the time to awaken to it. This is our call: to be patient, to become sensitive, and to not be afraid to intuit the flowing actions of the Spirit. When we do, in time, we are filled with unspeakable joy, ecstasies, peace and comfort.

All of these activities are both the beginning of an emerging Christianity in the world and anciently rooted in mystical praxes. If you begin to work with these techniques, mystical experiences will begin to arise. But more importantly, your heart will awaken and your life in Christ will begin to shine in new ways. Use these techniques to revolutionize your field or profession. Let the revelation come in order to change the world so that it might take on the characteristics of heaven. Remember that your true Self is one that is rooted within the Spirit of Christ. It is "I who no longer live, but Christ in me" (Gal. 2:20). It is in this place that we touch, unleash, and deepen our meditational excursuses. Starting here, in a place of rest, while engaging these various practices will open up an experiential dimension of one's union with Christ that is truly beyond anything anyone could ever put into words. Let these practices be a vehicle to take you into the Heavens and into the well of the Living Water that rests deep within our Hearts.

If you are interested in a weekly meditation group where we practice and learn an array of meditation fundamentals, and explore more advanced techniques together, visit **www.rooakh.com** for more information. Every week we meet online and get together to meditate.

We would love to see you there!

ENDNOTES:

i.   See www.aacetv8.com.

ii.   Also known as "out of body experiences," or OBE's.

iii.   On one level, the word "Spirit" engenders the idea that Divine in its totality *is* Spirit in perpetual becoming (John 4:24), while also stating that those who are united with Christ are an aspect of the Spirit's presence bodily (Romans 8:9-17) both in action and indwelling, like a temple (1 Cor. 3:16).

iv.   I borrow this term from A.E. Roberts. For more information on various procedures of sense making, see his journal publication, *The Side View.*

v.   These include but are not limited to:

- A belief in a transcendent and unmovable God that lives above and beyond creation. Sometimes this God is seen as something so perfect it becomes wholly static and never responds to the world, thereby making God totally non-relational. At other times, God is depicted like an all-powerful, Greek god sitting on a throne, waiting to pounce on those who sin, thereby creating a Caesar or tyrannical-like image of God that enables humans to be "okay" with humans who behave in a similar fashion according to this "divine" image.

- A belief that God not only knows the future perfectly but that God has orchestrated all events in the world according to Its will, thereby squashing free will and making God the author of all evil and suffering.

- An overemphasis on a *disconnected* hierarchical worldview of heaven based on positions of power, influence agents of control, which have led to oppressive structures of dominance.

- The doctrine of original sin and the presumption that all humanity is born as depraved creatures, as proposed by Augustine of Hippo in the 4th century. His doctrine created a fundamental bifurcation between God and the Human, which led to the devaluing and ignoring the fact that the Human was called good along with the rest of creation in Genesis 1.

- The doctrine of original sin doctrine also led to the theological doctrine of penal substitution that emphasized humanity's inherent separation from God. Thus, the only way to be on God's good side again was to enact the sinner's prayer, thereby alienating God to the world once again.

- The teaching that miracles and apostleship ended with the death of the first century apostles, which resulted in the worship of the Bible and programmed many to believe that the Spirit does not move or work in the world today.

- The concept that God inherently and exclusively manifests as masculine or male, which has led to a hierarchical male-centric system of control that disempowers and oppresses women.

- The concept that God is a white man, which has led to oppressive and destructive behaviors towards indigenous groups and peoples of color.

- An over-emphasis on heaven after death, which has led to malpractices of many within the Christian West to destroy the earth and its life giving environments.

- Literal readings of a new heaven and earth, as well as an obsession with the end of the world, rapture, and apocalyptic teaching that creation will be destroyed. This has led to a lack of empathetic and responsible environmental behavior, as well as care for nonhuman creatures on the earth.

- Luther's 16th century doctrine of sola-scriptura, or "scripture alone," which has led to the idolization of the written Bible and led to the loss of continual revelation as found in the world through nature and the life of the Spirit with those in Christ. This has led to dangerously strict and literalist interpretations of the texts that falter under any critical study, which causes for many who go down the path of study what some call a "crisis of faith".

- The Protestant tendency to read Jesus through the words of Paul, instead of reading the Pauline letters through the lens of the life and teachings of Jesus.

- Disregard for spiritual and life processes, which have led to a lack of understanding concerning grace and its role within our life and developed hyper-perfectionist tendencies within various parts of the church.

- Devaluation of mystical experiences and spiritual experiences in general as vehicles for the transformation of the human's Divine understanding.

- A lack of understanding of the Ecology of God both internally and externally.

vi.   For more on the history and structures of Jewish mysticism, see the works of Gershom Scholem, Moshe Idel, Rachel Elior, Pinchas Giller, and Daniel Matt.

vii.   Philippians 2:7, Hebrews 2.

viii.   When I mention the soul throughout this book, I do not assume it as an unchanging "substance" or even something one possesses, but rather the activity of life that generates one's becoming. As Spirit becomes, Soul becomes, as seen in Genesis 2. It therefore cannot be possessed or owned by oneself for it is the activity of existence and consciousness.

ix.   Hart, R., Ivtzan, I., & Hart, D. (2013). Mind the Gap in Mindfulness Research: A comparative account of the leading schools of thought. Review of General Psychology, 17, 453-466.

x.   Speca, M., Carlson, L. E., Goodey, E. & Angen, M. (2000), "A randomized, wait-list controlled trail: the effect of a mindfulness meditation-based stress reduction program on mood and symptoms of stress in cancer outpatients," Psychosomatic Medicine, 62, pp. 613–22.

xi.   Low, C. A., Stanton, A. L. & Bower, J. E. (2008), "Effects of acceptance-oriented versus evaluative emotional processing on heart rate recovery and habituation," Emotion, 8, pp. 419–24.

xii.   Kabat-Zinn, J., Lipworth, L., Burncy, R. & Sellers, W. (1986), "Four-year follow-up of a meditation-based program for the self-regulation of chronic pain: Treatment outcomes and compliance," The Clinical Journal of Pain, 2(3), p. 159; Morone, N. E., Greco, C. M. & Weiner, D. K. (2008), "Mindfulness meditation for the treatment of chronic low back pain in older adults: A randomized controlled pilot study," Pain, 134(3), pp. 310–19; Grant, J. A. & Rainville, P. (2009), "Pain sensitivity and analgesic effects of mindful states in zen meditators: A cross-sectional study," Psychosomatic Medicine, 71(1), pp. 106–14.

xiii. Davidson, R. J., Kabat-Zinn, J., Schumacher, J., Rosenkranz, M., Muller, D., Santorelli, S. F., Urbanowski, F., Harrington, A., Bonus, K. & Sheridan, J. F. (2003), "Alterations in brain and immune function produced by mindfulness meditation," Psychosomatic Medicine, 65, pp. 567–70.

xiv.   Hart, R., Ivtzan, I., & Hart, D. (2013). Mind the Gap in Mindfulness Research: A comparative account of the leading schools of thought. Review of General Psychology, 17, 453-466.

xv.   Ivanowski, B. & Malhi, G. S. (2007), "The psychological and neurophysiological concomitants of mindfulness forms of meditation," Acta Neuropsychiatrica, 19, pp. 76–91; Shapiro, S. L., Oman, D., Thoresen, C. E., Plante, T. G. & Flinders, T. (2008), "Cultivating mindfulness: effects on well-being," Journal of Clinical Psychology, 64(7), pp. 840–62; Shapiro, S. L., Schwartz, G. E. & Bonner, G. (1998), "Effects of mindfulness-based stress reduction on medical and premedical students," Journal of Behavioral Medicine, 21, pp. 581–99; Siegel, D. Mindsight: The New Science of Transformation (New York; Random House, 2010).

xvi.   Fredrickson, B. L. & Joiner, T. (2002), "Positive emotions trigger upward spirals toward emotional well-being," Psychological Science, 13, pp. 172–5; Fredrickson, B. L. and Levenson, R. W. (1998), "Positive emotions speed recovery from the cardiovascular sequelae of negative emotions," Cognition and Emotion, 12, pp. 191–220; Tugade, M. M. & Fredrickson, B. L. (2004), "Resilient individuals use positive emotions to bounce back from negative emotional experiences," Journal of Personality and Social Psychology, 86, pp. 320–33.

xvii. See, Dr. Danny Penman's Mindfulness an Eight-Week Plan for Finding peace in a Frantic World, for more information, p.5-6

xviii. The word "ritual" is one that has been castigated by American Protestants since it carries notions of repetition, practice, and routine, i.e. the qualities they reject within Catholicism. However, this rejection has thrown the baby out with the bathwater entirely and has propagated a subtle rebellion against the notion of ritualized practice altogether. As a concept, ritual is what facilitates ordered sacredness much like the groove on a record or an irrigation trench. They maintain and produce a sort of energetic memory that can become infused with Divine Spirit. When filled with intention and love, rituals can become one of the most beautiful aspects of our spiritual journeys.

xix.   Obviously there are exceptions to this, most notably the Quakers.

xx.   This is somewhat similar to the spiritual exercises created by Saint Ignatius of Loyola in the 16th century within the Jesuit tradition.

xxi.   Kaplan, Jewish Meditation, 41.

xxii. Kaplan, Meditation and the Bible, 64-65.

xxiii. See Pierre Hadot's What is Ancient Philosophy?

xxiv. Sherman, Partakers of the Divine: Contemplation and the Practice of Philosophy, 9.

xxv.   ibid, 10.

xxvi. Brock, *The Wisdom of Saint Issac the Syrian,* homilies 64, 65.

xxvii. Although Pseudo Dionysius popularized this approach, Saint Gregory of Nyssa was the first to widely introduce this technique through his seminal work *The Life of Moses.*

xxviii. We see this idea mentioned in Scripture, for example in John 1:18: "No one has seen or can see the Divine;" 1 Tim. 6:16: "He lives in unapproachable light;" Job 11:7-8: "His ways are unsearchable and unfathomable."

xxix. *The Cloud of Unknowing and Other Works* (Penguin Classics), 29.

xxx. *The Cloud of Unknowing and Other Works (Penguin Classics) 9.*

ABOUT THE AUTHOR

For the past eight years, Taylor Remington has cultivated and devoted himself to Christ-centered meditational and contemplative practices. The fruit of his experiences, insights, and studies have revealed and refined spiritual technologies that focus on aspects of feeling, intuiting, and sensing, which Taylor incorporates into his Rooakh practicum and teachings in order to reintegrate one's body, soul, relationships, and external world into unity with the Spirit. Through these Spiritcentric techniques, Taylor guides the individual into new experiences of the ever-flowing Spiritual life in Christ, which inevitably results in an embodied peace, or Shalom, in all areas of one's life.

Taylor has participated and served in multiple Christian spiritual arenas for the past ten years. He has a B.A. in Inter-Cultural Studies and a minor in Biblical studies from Biola University as well as an M.A. in Theology and Religion from the Claremont School of Theology, where his studies focused on transpersonal aspects of experience and becoming. Taylor has studied and served under Dr. Ogbonnaya of Aactev8 International for the past eight years learning and embodying both Christian and Jewish methods of Divine engagement. Taylor's background and expertise are centered around the Spiritual, as emphasized through the historical, mystical, philosophical, and theological practices and ideas of the ancient, medieval, and modern Church. In addition to his scholastic training, Taylor is a certified Mindfulness and Meditation teacher as well as a certified Christian Mindfulness teacher.

Taylor and his wife Megan currently live in Southern California and enjoy spending their time traveling, learning, reading, and watching the Lakers.

SeraphCreative

Heaven's Heart for Earth

Seraph Creative is a collective of artists, writers, theologians & illustrators who desire to see the body of Christ grow into full maturity, walking in their inheritance as Sons of God on the Earth.

Sign up to our newsletter to know about future exciting releases.

Visit our website :

www.seraphcreative.org

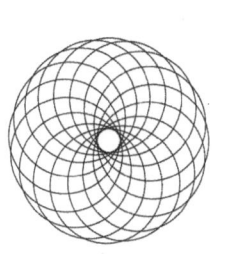

CPSIA information can be obtained
at www.ICGtesting.com
Printed in the USA
FSHW020508110920
73705FS